On Character and Mental Toughness

William James Moore

ISBN-13: 978-1494780050
ISBN-10: 1494780054

DEDICATION

For Amy, Shane, Hunterdon, Nolan, Grace, my parents John and Pat Moore, my in-laws Bill and Chris Tyburski, and my students and players.

You have all given me something to care about and made me better.

CONTENTS

ACKNOWLEDGMENTS

This book would not be possible without the sage wisdom and enduring friendship of Kevin Nagle and Ken Doyle, as well as the many other friends who have shared a portion of my journey. Likewise, the many fine educators I learned from and worked with including the staffs at North Hunterdon High School, the University of New Hampshire, Maine Central Institute, Glen Mills School, Princeton University, Springfield College, Western New England College, Agawam High School, Westfield High School, Vermont All-Star and National Football League High School Player Development. Thank you to Kristen Biancuzzo and Joe DeChristopher for kindly agreeing to read through this work. I am always grateful for the inexplicable tolerance and invaluable input of Amy Claire Moore.

FOREWORD

Are you on the path? Would you be the type of person that others would want to be in a fox hole with? Are you a person of honor? Are you looking for the easy path? Character and Mental Toughness is what Bill writes about in the following guide of honing. It will help you find clarity on the path you are currently treading. I have been honored to write the foreword of Bill's opus which is worthy of detailed study and practice. But before I tell you about me or why you should continue reading I would like to share with you some beauty from one of humanity's best poets which encapsulates the essence of this book.

I often share Robert Frost's *The Road Not Taken* with my clients and everyone knows the line "Two roads diverged in a wood, and I – I took the one less traveled by, and that has made all the difference." But for me the most impactful line in my life and business has been "Yet knowing how way leads on to way, I doubted if I should ever come back." I have repeated that line to myself and my clients 1000's of times. It has power and I suggest that you ponder it: That way leads on to way for once you start anything that action sets off a cascade of probabilities which will either serve you or hinder you. The choice is yours if you are "Aware" as Bill points out.

My name is Ken Doyle and I am the Founder of FinancialAdvisorCoach.com. Much like Bill I coach people to reach their potential but our arenas are much different. I help the elite in the business world become even more elite as my Uncle Rich used to tell people, "Ken helps rich people become richer." I have the benefit of choosing who I work with. Bill does not. I can fire my clients. Bill cannot. I can curse at my clients, call them dumb and reference every politically incorrect statement under the sun and not get in trouble for it. Bill on the other hand operates in a more constrained and politically correct environment. My only concerns are the results that my client produces. Bill's concern is the team, the community, the parents, his coaches, and his administrators. To put even more pressure on him he is also a public figure. I on the other hand am not. I cannot be fired. Bill can be. He is a man who operates in a field of immense pressure with many stake holders in the outcome of his team and he has orchestrated success by the ingrained tenets in this book which are also in his character.

I could not do what he has done and I am honored to write a few words on "The Way". I believe "The Character Way" is the bedrock of his success and will be the steel of your success.

Since you are reading this book you care. You care about yourself, your team, your company or your future! Good for you because as you read going forward "caring" is a trait of the Character Way

There are no guarantees in life but we can stack probabilities. For example going to college does not guarantee you will get a job but it does increase the probability of one. Going to class consistently does not guarantee you will get a passing grade but it does increase the probability of it. Practicing the "Character Way" does not guarantee success in your endeavors but it does increase the probability immensely.

This book will help you stay on your particular "field of play" if you choose to takes its lessons to heart because what my life has shown me is the "way does lead on to way" in all the things that you do. As a matter of fact, everything that you do counts. Everything that you do will either keep you on the field of play, shove you to the sidelines or throw you into the stands. Think deeply on this: If you are on the sidelines can you really affect the game being played? Worse yet what can you do from the stands? Being a spectator does not improve your play.

The Character Way will keep you on your Field of Play. The hard path becomes the easy path while the easy path eventually becomes the hard path. I know this from my own experience. It was HARD to leave Boston, my career and all my contacts to do a startup company in San Diego. It was hard to watch that company fail and take my personal finances down with it. It was hard staring a business with no salary, benefits or paid vacations. It was hard to build the business, pay the rent and buy food. It was hard to start a relationship and build a business with my girlfriend. It was hard to buy our first house. It was EASY to buy our second house. It was even easier to buy our first summer house. It was easy to add another business to our portfolio. It was easy to buy our third House. It was easy to buy our second summer home. It was easy to winter in Florida. This list can continue but when we began Getting Results Coaching in June of 2002 it was very hard as most people told us to get real jobs and that it was crazy to start a business with someone you are dating. Few people have a lifestyle like the one my girlfriend and now wife have created. Reading Bill's book helped me see which traits of my character helped me build the success that I have and it also highlighted some aspects of character that I need to continue to hone if I want to develop further.

When no one is looking is when your character will shine through. Hone it while you can. Do not be sloppy. Realize that everything that you do counts. Finishing this book and practicing the traits will count. Way leads onto Way! The Character Way will serve you. It is a hard path, and most will not tread upon that path. But if you should, way will lead on to way and it will make a world of difference for you.

Ken Doyle
Founder Getting Results Coaching
FinancialAdvisorCoach.com
Author – The Journey: An Evolution of a Financial Advisor

PREFACE

"Everyone thinks of changing the world,
but no one thinks of changing himself." -Leo Tolstoy

Who the heck am I to write a book? I am just a small town teacher and football coach. I have coached, taught and worked with people who went on to fame, but I am not famous. As I write this my notoriety is confined to the people I have known through my twenty years of teaching and coaching, my friends and family. Famous people write books or have books written about them; I know, my book shelves are filled with books of men and women who are well renown. Not surprisingly, many of these books were written by or about coaches. Coaching books are popular sources of information for people who want to go for the gold or carry their team to victory. Sports metaphors abound for a reason, most can relate to them. They appeal to anyone seeking to achieve, and empathize with those who fall short of the finish line.

Who the heck am I to try to influence your thinking then? Well, think about the people who have influenced you; the math teacher or baseball coach, your favorite aunt or uncle, a grandparent, a boss or co-worker, or even your parents and children. Very few people know of Sue Keller, Allie McGharen, Dick Messenger, George Greiner, Don Rissmiller, Nancy Brown or Angelo Correalli either. These people have changed our lives, yet chances are they were not all that famous. They simply said something or did something which had an indispensible impact on us. Their words changed our course of behavior or served as seeds of wisdom which blooms later in our lives. Their very presence in our lives allowed us to see how to go about our tasks and react in a given situation. They were the people we trusted enough to go to when we had to make a difficult decision or could not figure out why we were struggling. I hope I can become something similar to you; a teacher or coach or colleague who enters your life and makes an impact, large or small, for the better. I am humble enough to try and ask this of you, and confident enough to believe I have a few nuggets of wisdom that will help you answer the bell, get off the bench, make the all-star team and taste the fruits of victories large or small.

I am a winner, but also a loser. This is important, because just as you learn valuable lessons from losing so have I; and I have had profound losses. From my professional and personal experience I have learned valuable lessons that I want to pass on to you for the benefit of you, your loved ones, and your organization. These are the lessons I have passed on to my children, my students, and my players. These are the lessons I have shared with my fellow coaches, teachers and other friends who work in a broad array of professions. Their appreciation for my helping them make better decisions, recognize obscured opportunities, and find meaning and energy in their lives spurs me on to share these lessons with you.

My life and educational experience in a myriad of settings has taught me how to win and how to lose, and more importantly made me aware of their distinguishing contributing factors; many of which you may have not previously considered of consequence. These factors may be more readily identified, studied and applied to make a difference between success and mediocrity, mediocrity and failure, serenity and madness.

I have found these factors are universal. They can be applied at the individual level when looking at one's academic, athletic, relationship or work performance. They can be applied at a larger level when examining team or unit behaviors. They can be applied in analyzing organizational, business, or institutional performance. They can be applied, past or present, to broader societal issues such as climate change or national debts.

Near the end of *An Inconvenient Truth* Al Gore seems perplexed and frustrated because, when it comes to saving the world, he can't get as much done as he hopes. Why? Because the population, you, me and the other people we deal with everyday, lack character and mental toughness. Here is this huge complex global issue, articulated in an amazing and influential way, yet we struggle to progress because of our collective character and mental toughness issues. This is the hidden truth; character and mental toughness matter in everything we do and we need to develop the skills to recognize their importance. We need to be able to identify these traits, and respect the enormous role they play in our success and failure. With some effort we may learn how to master character and mental toughness to the point where we can see the vital role they play in our lives.

INTRODUCTION

"No more time arguing what a good man should be. Be one". - Marcus Aurelius

To come to hard fought conclusions that have been previously concluded is the measure of life's frustration. So much of our knowledge is arduously self-acquired when it could have been otherwise so readily won. Each day we hear or read something in repose that we have already learned in agony. We waste time navigating by trial and error and thus descend countless avoidable ravines. How much better off would we be if we had first taken pause to strengthen our being and acquire a more accurate and durable compass for life? How invaluable would it be to save the time and tears we tragically lose to our preventable missteps?

If you picked up this book there is a very good chance you want someone or something to succeed. Before we get rolling I want to congratulate you because you have taken an important step. You have taken the initiative to do something rather than continue complaining or ignoring the issues you and/or your organization face. Constantly complaining and ignoring issues are techniques of failure. They do little or nothing for you or others. By picking up this book you have demonstrated character. By reading this book, you will grow your character. By continuing to read this book when you would rather not and then ultimately finishing this book you will demonstrate mental toughness. By applying what you learn to everything you do, you will find understanding and excellence. You will be better for reading this and hopefully learn some pragmatic principles and techniques you can use to help others get better.

You will be a light of awareness that those without character and mental toughness can never envision.

Put a student with great character & mental toughness in nearly any classroom & they succeed to potential. The same goes for players and employees in their associated environments. The ones who consistently rise are the ones who have the character to do the work & the mental toughness to keep working no matter what. The challenge has little to do with a particular field or endeavor or practice. The challenge is to universally accelerate building of strength of character because that is the greatest controllable determinant of success or failure when looking beyond uncontrollable natural talent.

Character is so simple we overlook it and take it for granted. That does not make it any less powerful. That does not make it any less worthy of our attention, our mindset. We all know foundation as metaphor. The lack of character is a pervasive issue when absent or wanting in all foundations. It influences all you do and don't do and anytime you do it or don't do it. Its presence is the cause of your consistent achievement and its absence the reason for your most debilitating failures. Don't discount it. Don't believe it unworthy of your effort to master it and teach it to others.

When people say authentic it so frequently sounds disingenuous but being genuinely straightforward is an integral part of this book. In these chapters I will share with you quotes of celebrated and obscure wisdom. I will provide the occasional example of an archetype of each character trait. But, more frequently I will give examples of traits as I have encountered them in my experience. I will also ask you to think of your own archetypes and examples from your own experience. I probably don't have to do the latter as it will likely come naturally. So please consider this request a friendly call for reflection and not a nagging demand.

There are negative examples of each character trait and the archetypes that have lacked the character trait or have, to our horror, whole heartedly embraced the negative. However, I have purposely refrained from including these negative examples as much as possible. I want to celebrate the positive and not dwell on nor further illuminate the negative. There is value in looking at things from as many perspectives as possible, including the negative. For the most part I have included only that which will be of use in understanding the common consequences of not embracing the positive trait.

I am going to help you to identify and institute the means of success as it lies hidden in the plain sight of our everyday existence. It matters not whether you want yourself to succeed, a loved one to succeed, a student to succeed, an employee to succeed, a team to succeed, a business to succeed, or even your country to succeed. Success comes down to three factors beyond external serendipity; talent, character, and mental toughness. I hope to show you the latter two can be learned, can be controlled, can grow and develop. Likewise they can rot or go untapped. Above all, I want to show you they were once taught, are rarely taught now, and need to be taught again. Once you learn why they are important, you can work on them and then get the most out of your talent and the talents of others; your children, your players, your employees, and even your fellow citizens.

If we do this right, you are going to view the world, your life and the events you see and read about, through the lens of character and mental toughness. That vision and the ability to recognize the applications for that vision will enhance you and those you care about and rely upon.

1
CHARACTER ISSUES

"Of the Wrong we are always conscious, of the Right never."- Thomas Carlyle

Does everything happen for a reason, or do we reason everything that happens? The consequences of success or failure are huge. The reasons for success or failure are small. Parents can see their child's future brightened or dimmed when their child makes just a couple of whimsical decisions. The fortunes of companies are made or destroyed by the actions of a single employee with questionable integrity. Coaches are fired when just a few of their athletes do not perform close to their potential or make poor decisions off the field. Likewise, coaches can be fast tracked when an overlooked recruit develops to his full potential and leads the team to a great season. Relationships are strengthened or ruined when a partner takes a single passionate action. Even the sanctity of academia is changing as teachers increasingly are evaluated primarily on the performance of students they do not choose and cannot fire.

How often are you disappointed, or find you are complaining because something does not get done, or done right, or done on time? Think for a moment how often you hear yourself or others complain. If you are attuned, you hear complaining constantly. My fellow coaches speak of the lack of effort of their players. Fellow teachers talk about students not paying attention or doing their work. People speak of the lack of ambition, or initiative or a persistent and annoying sense of entitlement. My father complains incessantly about the clerks at the market, the driver on the road, the employee on the other end of a service call. My friends and family speak of their problems at work and at the mall.

Pick up the paper and you see instance after instance of someone screwing up their own life as they screw up those of other people. Turn on the news and hear about government at a standstill or moving forward without considering the long term ramifications of their actions.

These are not generational issues. The boorish and narcissistic, the lazy and arrogant know no bounds of age or place or situation. They are everywhere and we have all recognized they are growing more prevalent. It's not just good help that is hard to find; it is good, productive, trustworthy, and perseverant anything that is hard to find. Cut past the immediate details of these problems and you will find each of these to be an issue of character & mental toughness at the core.

There exists a larger struggle we are all, either willing or unwilling, participants in. Over time we experience or witness the larger war between toxic narcissism and character. This war is being waged in almost every realm (athletics, businesses, churches, schools, government, city streets etc.) where people interact. For those of us who are desperately rooting for character to prevail, we must not give into our frustrations, but rather should apply a pleasant, preventative dose of character vocabulary and positive example whenever possible.

I am afraid too many adults are like the ancient Greek hunter Narcissus himself in that they will never have an awareness of anyone's needs but their own. They will never get "it." Trying to legislate and confront every instance of ignorant behavior is futile. The narcissists are too emotionally immature to recognize their destructive behavior and too emotionally deprived to care. Worse, they are fed by attention, be it positive or negative, and enjoy lashing out at those who dare try to change or improve them. Rather, let us focus on preventing self-serving behavior from forming in the first place by helping our young people to realize the great joy of teamwork, selfless contribution, and awareness of others.

Begin by placing instances of positive and negative behavior into a larger framework of character. Help people understand almost every situation requires a decision they must make which has both positive and negative consequences and individual and group ramifications. Then empower those people to see they can grow in character by understanding the vocabulary and applying it to these situations they encounter during their daily lives.

Every day we are receiving confirmation the great Irish philosopher Edmund Burke was right when he wrote "All that is necessary for evil to triumph is for good men {and women} to do nothing." So please let us all take the initiative to get humble enough to recognize our own (and our children's own) character weaknesses and become disciplined enough to overcome them. Let us make character building a priority so all of the things we do will rise up and rest on its firm foundation.

Unfortunately, when it comes to character traits, we just assume other people know them. We assume people should know what we know. I have made this mistake many times. I have also been victim of this mistake many times; meaning people assumed I should know something about character, that I did not; or they mistakenly assumed something about my character.

"Is it not a false statesmanship that undertakes to build up a system of policy upon the basis of caring nothing about the very thing that everybody does care the most about? -a thing which all experience has shown we care a very great deal about?"
-Abraham Lincoln

Society is suffering from a failure to coherently teach character and most of our individual and group problems are traceable to that failure. Presented here is a highly effective, yet simple and inexpensive, process to teach character. Seeing the world through the spectrum of character, we discover most problems have a root cause (lack of character) and we have a viable means to correct the problem (pro-active character education or PACE).

Change the setting and you will find my experiences are similar to yours. You reach a point in teaching and coaching where you must adapt or move on. You have to change your pedagogy, as the raw material (students) you get is increasingly further away from the manufactured good (graduates ready for success) you are expected to produce. The old programming term GIGO (garbage in-garbage out) doesn't apply when we are talking about our children and the future of our country. Like you in your situation, we have no choice but to succeed.

Unfortunately, most educators and educational leaders have two fatal flaws that negate their ability to address this issue. They fail to grasp all of the variables of educational success and they are hopeless fad chasers. They will inevitably advocate a new program, which will bring sweeping changes. They will spare no expense of an educator's time and a taxpayer's dollar to see the implementation of their program. Most foolishly, the many people who care spend most of their time complaining because they recognize these fad programs won't change anything. This is incredibly frustrating because nobody seems to be addressing the true problems we are confronting.

I often tell my football players, "It's as if I can see the future." I tell them what will happen, and then to their great surprise my premonition will later be confirmed. An example of my clairvoyant prowess would be when I tell them "their way," usually a technique that is easy to master, will not lead to consistent success. They surely doubt me. I tell them "my way," a more difficult technique to master, will allow them to become consistently successful.

It is amazing how a couple hours on a Saturday morning spent watching the video of the previous night's game will confirm my superpowers. See, you really do stand a better chance to catch the ball if you use BOTH hands. That is a fundamental skill, yet it can cost my team or even the college or pro teams a championship if it is not executed. What happens in watching film of our games is that our player's perceived reality becomes much more attuned with reality, when confronted with a truth that is so obvious but was hidden to them.

So let me try to prognosticate our current situation. Here is my prediction for a pending discussion on a pending workplace problem. People will sit and mention issues with people. All kinds of issues like the ones I mentioned above. Someone will say "people these days" or "kids these days." Someone will bemoan a lack of effort. Another voice will convey an example of a lack of manners. Someone will say, "It's as if" and most of the attendees will nod their heads. Lots of examples of unsuitable behavior will be proffered. While each person speaks, the individuals present will schematically recall instances they have encountered which are quite similar, thus explaining the nodding heads. Some will reiterate points that have already been well made. We grudgingly accept they can't help themselves. All of these actions are beneficial, even admirable. Identification of the problems that exist is obviously critical to solving those very problems.

However, the conversation will then take a turn down a fruitless path, as those present have a solid handle on the parts but fail to grasp, or articulate the whole. Someone will mention school, workplace or societal rules. People will blame their fellow colleagues or community members, (aka SOME PEOPLE) and subtly convey their frustration with those in leadership roles. The leaders will diplomatically fault their charges for lack of enforcement of the rules. Both parties will then reach consensus that it's all someone else's fault.

There might be some mention of starting a committee. There will be some general conclusion we all need to do a better job, and each individual present will leave concluding "we" actually means everyone but themselves. Within weeks, and likely much earlier, everything will remain the same.

If this conclusion is acceptable to you, then read no further. If you are willing to invest in a possible solution, then read on. First we have to get our mind right. What is the nature of man; good or evil or both? I answer with another question; why do we have lockers at my high school or at your local gym instead of the cubby holes students had in elementary school?

I am pragmatic, I believe people are both good and evil, particularly young people who are the most susceptible to circumstantial change. As such, I believe people may be influenced towards one direction or the other. This catalyzes a belief that pro-active change is possible, particularly among young people.

The problem with my being a pragmatic, a realist, is that the optimists consider me to be a pessimist and the pessimists consider me to be an optimist. Forgive my tangent pre-refutation. Now, we may go on to our next great problem.

Where is the line to be drawn? Most schools have rules about cell phone use. Truth be told I personally could care less if a kid has a cell phone out during the passing time between classes, or checks to see if she has received a text once her work is completed. To some this position is absolute sacrilege; to others it is quite reasonable. Now if you want to spend all of your time arguing this point, you miss THE point.

The rules are already written. We are to enforce them and abide by them. We can debate what they should be or not be, but that is not the core of the problem. You have an opportunity to make a real difference in this moment, but if you are distracted by what the rules should be, you are going to waste a rare chance to adopt a new way of viewing the situations and events you encounter and witness.

In our schools, gymnasiums, and workplaces, every leader and constituent is well aware of the rules. Add, subtract or modify them all you want. But those rules don't seem to be getting us where we want to go do they? Rules are the perceived reality. They are not reality. Reality is a whole bunch of people choosing to do what is good for them in the short term. They are busy trying to get by with as little effort and inconvenience as possible instead of getting themselves and their organizations better.

A few years back I was having some health issues. The first was a low grade fever. I complained to my wife for weeks about this fever I just couldn't seem to kick. The other issue was that I had chills. The chills would not go away. I spent all my time bundled up and cold. Another problem was intense waves of stomach pain. I had other issues as well that would sometimes present simultaneously and other times present separately. Each one I would complain about.

After about a month, I finally gave in to my wife's requests and went to see a physician for the first time in a decade. He sent me for a CT scan. The three technicians were all fairly recent alumni from the school where I teach. They were nice kids. They told me that after the CT, they would forward my results to my physician and he would take it from there. I got out of the CT machine and all of three of the techs were standing there just looking at me through the window of the control room with rather expressionless faces. I waved good-bye and smiled. All three raised their right hands, but nobody smiled.

The next day I had a call from my physician. Long story short, I had cancer. I had surgery. I have been fortunate so far.

My point is just like the lousy patient I am, we all complain about the symptoms. People (parents, students, players, employees, leaders etc.) are lazy. People are tardy. People cheat. People are disrespectful. People are clueless about the correlation of effort and result. People don't prepare for obvious consequences. People disturb others. People constantly seek the easiest path, not the most beneficial path. People have no long term goals. People lack direction. People curse.

Do we have corrupt politicians? Do we have unethical business people? Do we have people who cut you off in traffic or endanger the lives of others with their recklessness? Do people selfishly take advantage of the kindness of others? Do people abuse authority? Do people slander other people anonymously through media? Do people tell half truths? Do people do stupid and self-serving things? Is there not someone without a child parking in the "parent with infant" parking spot while they run in and purchase 17 items in the 12 item or less line?

I assert these are symptoms. They are not the problem. These are symptoms of a lack of character. The problem is a great many of these people have never been taught character or taught well enough.

Next, we try to treat the symptoms. My wife gave me plenty of Tylenol and ibuprofen to help me with my fever and chills. It helped for a bit, but then the symptoms came back. She could have given me a boatload of drugs; those symptoms would keep coming back and would have gotten worse. I didn't have fever and chills. I had cancer. Likewise, we try to treat the symptoms too. We lecture the lazy and confront the bad. We give kids detention and send adults to lock up. We write up our employees. We have heart to heart talks. We give people stern looks of disapproval. When we tire of ineffective treatments, we do our damndest to ignore the issue until we just can't take anymore. Then we storm the boss's office or rip the team or send the strongly worded email. We feel like we will continue to suffer indignities if we don't confront the issue so we try again.

So let me review. We all can identify the symptoms. We all can treat the symptoms. Treating the symptoms is ineffective, because the symptoms are not the problem.

So might we be better off in identifying the source of the symptoms, i.e. the problem? Then, once we identify the problem we obviously need to explore a remedy. Is our problem our own students, players, family members and colleagues? Is our problem only our own or only found in our town or state or country, or is it rather a much larger problem than we initially realize?

Ok Coach, you say, I am with you. These are issues we are all dealing with all the time, in every setting and they are all symptomatic of a global problem, so what is the remedy?

Well hold on a minute. What is the best way to fight a disease? Is it better to suffer the symptoms, and then introduce expensive and time consuming treatments or is it better to inoculate against the disease? Instead of reacting to these symptoms one by one, issue by issue, would it not be smarter of us to prevent them from emerging by preventing the disease which causes them? There is no magic shot which will prevent these problems, and their manifestations, but there is something powerful we can do and it's cheap, expedient, and effective.

Though trial and error is a highly effective learning technique, it's rather horribly inefficient and painful. Yet, this is the pedagogical realm to which we have exiled character education. Imagine if we taught math, science, and language solely when they came up as a result of some other random and unrelated activity.

Rather than react to each moment character presents itself, we need to become pro-active. The cure I propose fits in well with what we do best. Educate and learn. Education is a powerful force. Education freed the slaves. Education created civil rights. Education led to a man on the moon and the vaccine for polio (remind me to update my cliché list). Education led to the enlightenment, and the freedoms and liberties we have been blessed with. Education is more powerful than violence and despotism combined as evidenced by how, through the modern age, we have increasingly had less of each.

We are born ignorant. That may not be pleasant to hear, but does that make it untrue? Ignorant means not knowledgeable or unaware. At birth we are totally dependent and totally selfish. We certainly have instincts, but we don't truly know anything. All we know is what we want. We want to be fed. We want our diapers changed. We want to be burped. We want hugs. Babies are all about themselves; me, me, me. Infants don't care if others need sleep, or if others have something which needs to be done. Infants only care about their own needs.

As we are educated in school, in sports, in our families and communities, we are, in reality, becoming less ignorant. We are becoming more enlightened. This education allows us to become aware of the concerns and needs of people other than ourselves because someone teaches us. We soon learn perspectives other than our own. When faced with such education we have a choice in life. We can choose to remain ignorant or we can choose to become enlightened. Remaining ignorant is easy. Do nothing challenging. Learn little. Listen less. Do whatever you want. Question nothing you currently believe. Worry only about your own wants and needs in the immediate moment.

Becoming enlightened is difficult. Take on as many challenges as you can. Learn all you can. Investigate if there is a better way. Recognize there are other people in the world. Become aware of their wants, their needs, their accomplishments. Rise to the challenge of each new day and its whispers for you to get further away from the person you were the day before.

Our problem is not so much an unwillingness to become educated in character as it is the lack of opportunities available to directly and methodically learn character. We have great swaths of our population that simply and tragically have never been offered a chance to learn character in a formal setting or been taught through reading, lecture, video, and the like. In short, we would all be better off if kids were told they had to sit down and learn this in a classroom setting. We would all be better off if adults were made aware they had missed an important piece of their character education but can pick up a book or attend a discussion.

People smoke fewer cigarettes these days. This is because our youth were taught the dangers of smoking. Those kids went home and confronted their smoking parents and grandparents. Adults were further reached through public service advertisements, and the efforts of countless individuals who spoke out against smoking any chance they could. We need this same effort in regards to character.

There is really only one way to consistently succeed in all areas of your life and that is tie your actions to your aims. The way to do that is to have character and mental toughness. The Character Way teaches us to consider others needs and our own future. It is the means to shared and sustainable success. So we need to teach people before they step onto the field, or get behind the wheel or talk to someone, they have an important choice to make. They can remain ignorant or become enlightened. They will make that choice every time they walk into a classroom, or suit up for work, or get on the road or interact with others in person or online. Rather than be reactionary and sit back as people find that out for themselves, let us teach them!

Stop complaining. Stop ignoring. Instead, start going to war for your own heart and mind as well as those of your children, your students, your players, your employees, and your fellow citizens. We each serve on the front lines of fighting ignorance and must engage in the fight to enlighten the masses. Stop the complaining and ignoring and start the learning, teaching, and personal example of character. You will see those things you complain about and have to ignore in order to keep your sanity will dissipate.

Start learning character. Start viewing problems as character problems. Start teaching others character first and foremost before you teach them specific skills. Start recognizing that when they are making a mistake in their field or endeavor it is likely a character mistake.

Not everyone will listen. Not everyone will act. But you will reach more than you think and you will profoundly change lives. As a result, you, your students, your players, your employees, your children and hopefully your community will start getting better and stop getting by.

Character is not an antiquated sentimentality; it is a necessary ageless imperative. Some believe things happen for a reason and timidly accept their fate; the strong reason what happens recognizing their role in the causes of their triumphs and failures and set about forging the best from their experience.

2
MY CHARACTER STORY

"A man's character is his fate." Heraclitus

Within seven years I had 30 court appearances related to my divorce; I went bankrupt, and was twice homeless and without a car; I had my eldest children moved three states away, then had them taken eight states away; I started another family I was obviously not ready for nor worthy of; I was diagnosed with cancer and had an organ removed; I succumbed to multiple addictions; I was diagnosed with a chronic incurable disease; I was hobbled by a grotesque dislocation; (things were much worse than I can write here). I was on the precipice of losing my career, my home, my family and my sanity. Unfortunately, that's where many of us find change. We reach the point of unbearable, where impossible to move meets impossible to stay. Our skin crawls, we are sick to our stomachs, we are in a perpetual state of anxiety we can no longer endure. It is only then that we take action. The action I took was to build my character.

The character lessons I learned allowed me to accomplish much in that time. I started my own seasonal small business and found new and rewarding jobs. I helped resurrect two dormant athletic programs and won four championships; firsts in the history of one program, firsts in a generation in the other. I started four athletic camps. I published articles. I was nationally recognized as a coach and three times nationally recognized as a teacher. I was given opportunities to be a public speaker and clinician. I survived cancer and was cured of an incurable disease. I have overcome addictions and learned to live a life of moderation. I have become a good father to my children near and far. I have become a worthy husband to an amazing wife; a better son, and friend. I have taught, coached, and inspired many. Now I hope to wake each day remembering my character is only as good as it is today.

Starting in the winter of 2007, I spent a great deal of time discussing character. I did this for a few reasons. The first was that our football program had a long run of mediocrity and failure during most of the 1990s and early 2000s. The program hit a low point in 2000 and 2001 winning only one game in two years. At that time the program was ranked 2nd to last in the state. The other high school in town was ranked last. The state of football in our community was literally as bad as it gets.

I started coaching at this school the following year and was charged with restoring respectability and competitiveness in the program. I will never forget the superintendent closing his door during my interview and telling me "Although I am hiring you to teach, and I would deny this publicly, your foremost mission is to coach football and turn around the program." I had secretly been given a quite public mission.

After slowly building the program back to a winner by 2005, we were disappointed to see our program unable to maintain that success in 2006. More importantly, we were still nowhere near making the post-season. Our offense had been very successful, but we still lacked commitment in the weight room. We also lacked mental toughness in finishing games and working through the discomfort of fatigue and pain. Every practice was a chore to coach because our effort and focus were lacking. Our players rarely strayed far from the easiest path. They utilized their natural abilities but too few enhanced them with off season training and intensity in practices. Our kids seemingly topped out as freshmen and were passed by kids at other schools who worked hard to develop their skills, physicality, and athleticism. Too many of our players relied solely on natural ability and a casual effort. In short we had nice kids, they just didn't know how to be winners.

"A fall into a ditch makes us wiser."-Chinese Proverb

As a staff we tried everything. I yelled a lot. I broke things. I did a lot of cursing. It may have kept us from going back to being winless, but it couldn't get us over the hump. Our coaching staff came back from practices and games always repeated the same phrase, "They just don't get IT." In the back of my mind I started to think about "It". What was "It?" How could I teach "It?" For the first time since I took over the program we had even lost our annual Thanksgiving Day rivalry game. It was really difficult to figure out how we had such a disappointing season because we had some great kids, but we just never could find a way to get our players to get "It" together.

"Character, not circumstances, makes the man"- Booker T. Washington

At the end of that 2006 season I was really desperate. To be honest I struggled as more than just a coach. I was having a rough time in just about every area of my life. When I say rough, I mean failing in just about every area imaginable, and suffering the inevitable rock bottom type of consequences.

But for some reason, I am a really bad quitter. I always feel like I lose because I'm not smart enough to figure out how to win before the clock says 0:00. I believe there is always a way to win, and if you give me enough time for my work ethic to wear the opponent or problem down, I will find a way to prevail. I know that's not necessarily true, that sometimes we are truly unable to win a situation, but that mentality of finding a way to win has served me pretty well through the years. After that season, that inability to give up was truly all I had left.

Up to my desperation point, or maybe a couple of years before as failing is rarely a sudden deadly fall but rather a gradual decline, I had lived a successful life. Things just always seemed to work out for me. My undergraduate education was paid for through an athletic scholarship. I earned a graduate fellowship. I had an attractive young wife, beautiful healthy children, a house in an affluent suburb, and noted success in my profession.

One Thursday night I ruined my life; again. Friday morning I woke up at a rest area in a borrowed car quite deservedly homeless; with my last $500, and no credit at all. I had two elder sons I didn't get to see much and a new son was heading that same way. I had a poor performing sports program I was in charge of and couldn't seem to fix; and my friends and family had already been through the ringer with me so much I simply couldn't burden them again. By Friday night I was in a cheap motel alone, fully knowing the damage I had done and as desperate as a person can be. Saturday morning I got up. I picked up a free newspaper and tried to find a car and a place to live. If I didn't find those things quickly, I would lose my job, which was about the only thing I had not ruined. I made a call about a car which cost $400. I made another call about a room for $100 a week. By Saturday night I had a small musty room to live in, a car which barely ran and some hope.

Two friends, both of whom knowing what it is like to start over and over, were willing to give me 15 minutes apiece to walk and talk. Sunday morning I went to the cathedral downtown, knelt in the back pew prior to mass, listened to a somber voice sing hymnals, put my face in my hands and uncontrollably wept. I knew I had negative options, but in that moment I found the only positive way out. I committed to humble myself and do whatever I could to make things as right as I could, not for myself, but for my family and others. My life was over. I now lived for others.

After mass I walked down the street to the YMCA and asked the receptionist if she had any information on recovery meetings and at that moment a middle aged man walked around the corner. He overheard what I had asked and he pulled me aside. He told me he was in recovery. We exchanged numbers and that night I went to a meeting with him. I had never realized how many problems within I had accumulated over the years until I could name them and started to tackle them. Six months of effort to straighten myself out followed. I discovered that despite my many achievements, my character was weak. I began to face my actions, and the decision process behind them. Things got better. Eighteen months after that Thursday night I was celebrating the birth of the most gorgeous daughter in the world. All I could think was that I was finally worthy of a daughter.

Only a few days after her birth I had an accidental discovery that saved my life. An unrelated health problem led to a CT scan that discovered the cancer which, undetected, would have killed me. Things had improved at work as well. My sports program finally turned the corner and made it all the way to the state championship game. We lost. Things improved but were never perfect. More success followed at home, and at work. It was never easy. Along the way follow up tests related to my cancer led to my being diagnosed with a chronic, incurable disease.

Yet almost a year later it disappeared. Tests showed no signs of it remained. I also had to deal with my eldest sons being moved from three states away where I could visit them once a month, to eight states away where I would rarely see them. Yet we remain close and I have found a way to still be their father and help guide them through their adolescence. We do not dwell on the fact that things are not the way we want them to be; instead we make the best of our times together. Through it all, I found a peace which comes solely from knowing you have already done well enough for others. That is not to say that I do not hope to do more. I try to do so every day.

I am a man of spirit, but I teach in a public school and fully respect the separation of church and state. I am not here to deny my faith, but I am not here to discuss it either. Instead I have found a way to teach some universal truths we can all agree on, regardless of culture or country or point of view. By maintaining that neutral state, I have come to a means of sharing my own transformation, and similar changes I have been able to ignite and/or recognize in others. Each day I hope to again realize my character is only as good as it is today.

I write and speak not for attention, but to try to make a difference large or small. I was able to turn my life around, so I know others can.

I try to make myself available and look for ways to reach people at the moment which is right for them. I plant seeds where I can, knowing they do not always bloom in the immediate. The vast majority of the details of my story are discussions for another day. Instead let us focus on the lessons, and I will share what I can of my experiences as it relates to that end. I do not want anything to get in the way of inspiring you, and helping you find peace and success; a perpetual combination we sometimes call fulfillment.

"Forming characters! Whose? Our own or others? Both. And in that momentous fact lies the peril and responsibility of our existence."-Elihu Burritt

As I began to pick myself up, I reached out for help. I had always read books, but I knew I had to go further. I got humble and asked for help. I asked guys I knew who coached, and not just football. I asked people I knew in other fields outside of coaching. I reviewed the many History books I had accumulated as a Social Studies teacher. I scoured every magazine and website I could find for a hint at what differentiated the consistently successful. I would even strike up conversations with strangers for the sole intent of understanding what made one person fail and another person succeed. I began to look all around me, all the time. I was alert to anything and everything which could be used to help me rebuild myself and the program.

I discovered what I had been asking of the players was correct. What was wrong was my method; my means of articulating what I expected from them. At the same time, I began to find I had not been living up to my own potential as much as I thought. I could do better in a lot of areas of my life. Ultimately, both the kids and I needed to work on our character. The problem was how to convey these lessons I had learned and wanted the players to learn as well.

My time with the players is limited by the governing body of state athletics. I couldn't call and participate in more than one off-season team meeting, but it was January and we had a lot of work to do if we were going to have any hope in September. I couldn't cram everything they needed to learn into the two weeks of pre-season before our first game. No, these guys had to start working on the mental aspect of their game immediately. Until that got straightened out, it would just be more of the same. I struck upon a plan and began to implement it that January. The state rule said I couldn't meet with them, but it didn't say I couldn't write to them. It also didn't say they couldn't meet on their own. I put together a binder and gave it to one of the seniors-to-be. I explained how important the contents of that binder were. I told him that later on that week, before our weight room hours, he would have to have a team meeting in an area near the gym which had a little bit of privacy to it. At that meeting he would remind everybody of our core beliefs and then share some quotes or a short piece of reading which he found inspiring. He then would say a couple of words and hand the binder to someone else, who would lead the group the following week. These meetings were only about 20 minutes long, but the players, to their credit, really took them to heart.

Most of the players went, sometimes even asking their winter sport coach if they could be a little late for practice for a "football meeting." I tried to call these things 1st and Ten meetings as they were in the first part of their training and we were trying to get our minds right first before we did anything else. Well we all came to call it our mental training, and the guys carried it out through the winter months until they all headed for their spring sports. At the same time, I began to set aside things that I came across that I thought might benefit the team. It could be a quote, or short story, or newspaper article, or a list, or a letter which I would write. But each week I would pull all of that stuff together, simplify it a bit to make it easier for high school students to understand, and then give it to the players' homeroom teachers to give to the players in the morning. So began our football team's character education program. Here is one of those first letters I sent to my team in January of 2007. I started very simply by saying this:

Character is the foundation on which success is built. Not just football success, but success in school, at work and at home. Putting some effort into having good character pays off in a huge way. It leads to better relationships, higher grades, promotions, and of course athletic success. None of us is perfect. We all have strengths and weaknesses in our character. But an introduction or a little refresher on character helps us become better.

In many ways a football game is a contest to see which team has the greater number of good people; people who worked hard in the off-season and in practice, learned their plays and techniques, practiced hard every day, overcame challenges etc. A state test is similar, as it is a contest to see which school has the greater character among it's student population. The same holds true of businesses. None of us is perfect, nor will we ever be perfect. But I hope you take the time to read what I will be sending you the next few weeks and see areas where you can improve as a person during your day at school, at home, at work, or in another sport.

These are lessons I have started to share with my sons because I want them to be successful and feel good about themselves and what they achieve in life. I care enough about you to share them with you. I hope you take the time to learn a little, and always recognize and accept when someone is helping you to become a better person. Like everyone else I need to work on some things too! What is Character? Character is made up of a combination of character traits; like humility, caring, discipline, etc. The stronger you are in those character traits the stronger your character will be. The stronger your character is, the more you will make the smart choices which lead to success.

When admissions counselors review your college application, employers interview you for a job, teachers evaluate you in class, or your coaches decide who is the next guy to get on the field, your character in different situations gives them a glimpse of who you are and who you might become. There are many attributes that contribute to your individual character. Building these attributes can help give you a stronger character, allow you to make better decisions and make you a more successful person.

So how do you build character? We used to learn it through experience; mostly by overcoming adversity. It was also reinforced by people throughout the community. Fewer kids each year face much adversity. There is usually plenty for them to eat, a roof over their heads, decent clothes on their bodies and enough electronics to keep them occupied. My kids are no different. But for all they have gained in comfort, they have lost something for not having to overcome discomfort, pain, and inconvenience. They are missing out on some valuable character lessons. It is as if they are eating plenty, but missing some important nutrients. Character lessons are the vitamins which supplement what we are missing in our daily diet of activities.

"Character cannot be achieved in ease and quiet. Only through experience of trial and suffering can the soul be strengthened, ambition inspired and success achieved."
- Helen Keller

Also, people were increasingly discouraged from teaching character in the community. Now if a kid does something that shows a lack of character, a member of the community is frowned upon from stepping up and teaching that kid a difficult lesson. Don't believe me? Next time a kid shows a lack of character at Walmart, speak up. See how his or her parent reacts. Parents these days tend to be protective first, sometimes to the detriment of a kid who could use a valuable character lesson. In addition, for some odd reason we teach character as a hidden part of curriculum. We teach it as part of something else. For example, character is an important part of high school and collegiate athletics, but we rarely say that outright. We never tell a kid he is signing up for the character team. We tell him he is signing up for soccer and, yeah by the way there will be some "life lessons" along the way.

We teach character through clubs, and music programs and in assemblies. We convey character lessons in our classrooms. But we never outright frame our character curriculum. We take it for granted that it just gets done. We just assume it is a foregone conclusion. We stumble for words when it comes to character pedagogy. We cloud our character lessons by mixing them within our activities and using an endless array of character related terms. "It" used to just be something you learned along the way, but that doesn't happen much anymore. Previously, many people learned character by regularly attending religious services. But people are increasingly less likely to attend such services. In addition, parents are busy working long hours and understandably exhausted when they are home. They spend less time with their kids than they would like. Likewise, we had an ever growing belief in not interfering in the lives of others, even when that interference might do some good. The result is character lessons don't get taught as much in a secular, hard working society. Like our long lost abilities to survive in the wild, many of these character lessons are being forgotten.

Many of us work at desks facing a screen the majority of our day. So what do we do to compensate? We go to the gym, we run or bike, we buy workout equipment and videos. We get some exercise during the day as we try to take the stairs rather than the elevator, but the bottom line is we schedule time to get our workouts in. We create an artificial situation to compensate for what is missing in our daily routine.

This is the same as character building. We simply don't face the daily character building adversities. So we must create situations and schedule times when character can be studied and learned. We must develop the apparatus to teach those character lessons.

We are all well aware that kids who are enrolled in sports tend to do well later in life. This is because those athletic experiences help teach character, not because the kid played basketball rather than hockey. My point is that it's the character building not the specific sport which builds the character that is most important. So why don't we formally teach character in our schools?

"Intelligence plus character; that is the true goal of education" Martin Luther King

We teach our subjects, but do we teach character? Character must be taught; actively and blatantly. Our current method of teaching by osmosis is terribly inefficient. Why not put character at the forefront? That's what I began to do when I took this very important thing which we hope people learn along the way, but obviously were not, and made it the most important thing that we do. How do you teach character in our times? The same way you teach most things: reading stories, reviewing vocabulary, discussing the topic with peers, watching videos etc.

Once I began to distribute these little lessons on what I believed were the most important character traits to my players I felt it was important to have a step by step progression. It was also important to boil down the plethora of redundant traits to a few core traits. In the morning players would receive one or two pages from me which contained an important character lesson. Some kids disregarded them, but most of our kids took something good from them.

Either way, I felt as though I were planting many seeds which I would continue to help grow. Just like in the classroom, I gave an overview, defined the key terms, incorporated excerpts from books or articles which I had read, and spoke from the heart. I started teaching what I believed was a unique step by step process in teaching character. Some teachers approached me, and began to confess they had read these lessons and thought they were a good thing. Within a few years, a group of teachers and administrators started a school-wide character education program. There was a character "word of the month," which was placed on banners and posted in every classroom in the school. Large character word banners were put up on the walls of our gym. There was also a character quote of the day which one of our class leaders would read for us during morning announcements.

Our campus community was slowly adopting a common character vocabulary which could be used during academic lessons and during our social interactions. Those words came alive as we applied them to our subject areas and conversations. My hope was that we would continue to grow in this area. I hoped teachers and coaches would become less upset by "kids these days," and move away from frustration to what we do best; educate. Then obviously, I hoped more kids in school would begin to see the benefits of having strong character, just as my players had. Likewise, I hoped more parents would recognize their kids' character growth just as my players' parents had.

I hoped our teachers would get beyond the poor parenting argument, and the parents would get beyond the bad schools argument and all of us would recognize if we focus on building the character of the kids, they will do better in every area of their lives (academic, athletic, citizenship, relationships etc.). Ultimately, I hoped we would begin to recognize each instance of poor behavior we see on the news and in our personal lives, on whatever scale, as simply another instance of the character void. Complaining about these instances accomplishes nothing. Education can do darn near anything. Character education is the empowerment we need to solve many of these problems before they appear.

"Nature magically suits a man to his fortunes,
by making them the fruit of his character."-Ralph Waldo Emerson

The first season after we started our character education program, our football team made it to the post-season for the first time in twenty years. We made it all the way to the state final. The next year we had the best regular season record in over twenty years and once again made it to the state final. Outside of football, I was doing great too!

I wanted to grow our efforts out into the greater community, not only in the town I taught in but in the neighboring towns as well. I wrote open editorial pieces for the local paper. I also started putting character related pieces on my school sponsored teacher webpage. A great many people would pull me aside, between classes, in the stands at sporting events, or even when I was taking the trash out to the end of my driveway. When they did, they were always appreciative of these efforts to promote character. My teacher page began to get views from around the country and around the world. I even received emails from people who read the pieces I put up on this webpage. This positive feedback was occurring on a one on one basis, and further spurred my efforts.

I brought an NFL program to our area. This program was free for all participants. Courtesy of the NFL, we could provide two hours of character education and eight hours of football instruction to high school football players from throughout the region. We began to reach 250 kids each summer. We had guest speakers, classroom sessions, and a planner for each player which contained pointers on character

Unfortunately, that's also when I started to recognize my character education push was beginning to falter. Enthusiasm for the character program at my school began to wane. There were no longer morning announcements or a character word of the month banner.

Our group of teachers and administrators that initiated the program no longer met. Soon it was just me, the character quotes I contributed to the morning announcements and the banners, which remained in the gym and many of the classrooms. While we still had many other terrific programs for the kids, the character emphasis was dissipating.

Likewise, I had a class of players come through with many who had very little interest in learning about character. They had slight humility and some of their parents had even less. These players had little interest in the traditions and successful routines we had worked hard to build. When the upperclassmen and coaches tried to push them to conform to our process, they had trouble seeing why they should. Of course, this was reflected in our on field performance and after two district championships we had back to back losing seasons in football and failed to make the post-season in lacrosse for the first time in years.

Ironically, the NFL program we ran continued to grow and a few of the other schools that had great levels of participation in the program began to see tremendous success on the field. These players from other schools would travel a half hour or more to get to our school for the NFL program. Many of these other schools had great levels of talent, but had previously fallen short of playing to their potential. Their wholehearted embrace of character had transformed them into consistent winners.

These other teams were listening and working hard. However, some of my own players literally lived across the street but would not attend the program. It was then that I decided to make some moves. I had complete faith in the character pieces I had to offer. I saw how successful people were when these lessons were acknowledged and applied. I saw how unsuccessful people were when they were not accepted nor acted upon. I took down all of the character pieces I had posted on my school provided teacher page. I stopped contributing quotes to the morning announcements. I didn't want to force my efforts on a seemingly disinterested faculty and student body.

So I decided to spend less time on trying to teach people who didn't want to learn and more time trying to find the people who did. I needed to find people who would recognize and appreciate what these lessons could do for them, their teams, their families, and their organizations. I started my own blog, unaffiliated with my school and my team. I put up the pieces I had previously written and shared with my team. I also put up new pieces as I put them together. As I came across books, poems, videos, and articles that taught aspects of character I put links to them on my new webpage.

I shared the pieces I wrote with my friends and former students and players on Facebook. I opened a Twitter account and shared links to the pieces I had written or come across. The feedback from the people on Facebook was fantastic. People I went to high school with told me how they were sharing the character lessons with their children. Guys I had crossed paths with in coaching told me how they were sharing the pieces with their own high school and college teams. My former players and students seemed to appreciate some good words from an ole' coach were still available to them as they transitioned to college and work.

Through my Twitter and blog I began hearing from parents, coaches, writers, business people, and wellness professionals who were sharing these lessons with their children, players, employees, and clients. I made my current players and their parents aware of both the blog and Twitter account, so the ones who were interested could find them. Many of the players and parents gave me amazing feedback. Of particular interest were the parents who pulled me aside or emailed me telling me they began to use these lessons to fuel their own pursuits of business or fitness success. I was also happy to see many of the students at school, some of whom I never even had in class, had also found my blog and Twitter contributions and used them to improve their athletic and academic performance. From all these sources I received very touching and heartfelt appreciation for what I had presented and what I was trying to accomplish. Their words, and their taking the time to pull me aside or send me a note, have inspired me to continue both studying character and passing on what I have learn along the way.

Not everyone is going to recognize the role of character, and the powers of pro-active character education. This is something I must reluctantly accept. However, I have been able to reach a great many and have been blessed to be able to help them achieve positive outcomes. Even better, those who grow strong character and mental toughness will pass those lessons on to their families, friends, neighbors and colleagues. I am grateful for the difficulties I encountered both professionally and personally, which have allowed me to see the power of character and mental toughness. I am grateful to be in a position where I can pass those lessons on to you, or help you reaffirm what you have already discovered. I encourage you to proactively teach character first and foremost. It will provide the firm foundation you need for sustained success for both you and your organization.

The Character Way is all uphill. It can seem grueling as it breaks you down and seemingly takes forever, but its beauty can only be witnessed from the views of its ascent.

The Easy Way is all downhill. It is always so seductive as it gives you what you want when you want it, but it will never keep you happy long or make you stronger along its many paths of descent.

3

THE CHARACTER WAY

"Everyone has the obligation to ponder well his own specific traits of character"-Cicero

The content of your character is largely determined by how content you are with what your current character has allowed you to achieve. It matters not if you find yourself in a hole or wish to avoid one; if you find yourself at a summit or wish to scale one.

Anyone can take The Easy Way and fail. Likewise, anyone can take the Character Way and succeed. Most people unwittingly bounce between the two and find themselves average. Day after day those Character Way vs. Easy Way decisions power you to your future, just as they have plopped you in your present predicament.

When you make each decision based on what you feel in the moment you fail yourself and others. Instead take The Character Way and serve yourself and others well. Once you learn how much character and mental toughness play into your success and failure, your families, your teams and your businesses, you begin to take responsibility for your life.

Here is a pragmatic answer. This invaluable process and perspective, you can utilize, teach, model and apply to all areas of your life. Here is how to gain that narrow margin and prevent that single instance of destructive behavior which can topple your life, your team, your career, or your company. Here are the steps you can begin to climb, or begin to climb again. Here is the way to actually reach your potential and help others to do the same. Here are the lessons you, your children, your players, and your company need to advance and maintain all previous advancement. Here is a universal means to success. Here are some of the infinite lessons of The Character Way.

Character building is a continuous process. We generally take a little from our experiences each day and try to use these little blocks of knowledge to further strengthen and build our character. I think this is how most of us go about initially building our character. This can be effective, yet it is rather inefficient and haphazard. Such a method would be better applied to a well developed character rather than a developing one.

In all my years of coaching and teaching it seems there is a natural progression in which character is built in individual players (people) and teams (groups). Likewise, one must be disciplined in not using too many terms interchangeably with their synonyms. A strict focus on the eleven core character traits, articulated in this specific way, allows one to recognize them, study them in depth, and communicate and adopt them effectively. The traits should then be perpetually reinforced as we recognize and apply them when they present themselves in our individual or shared experience.

The purpose of introducing and studying the traits in my suggested manner is so we can efficiently recognize and apply them as we seek our purpose and pursue our goals. I have written a piece on each individual core trait, sharing stories and quotes which will help in better understanding the core traits and their benefits. In learning the traits, I suggest spending a formal weekly or monthly session reviewing each trait. This can be done as a group or on an individual basis. Then as instances of that trait present over the course of that period further reflect and address them. This allows for the study of a single core trait in depth while focusing on that trait as it relates to your own environment. Once the core traits are studied continuously look for ideas which will further strengthen them within yourself and your organization. Three things are likely to happen as you go through this process. First, you will likely hear something new. Second, you will likely hear something you already know. Third, you will likely hear a new perspective on something you already know.

The steps of building character are the same as those I have written and shared with my teams, my children my colleagues and my friends. In addition to the pieces on the eleven core character traits, I will also share specific pieces I have written to clarify and reinforce them. For now, consider this an outline and overview. By no means will I consider what I share with you authoritative or exhaustive. I will simply be sharing what I know of each particular trait in an effort to establish a core from which to grow, reflect on, and approach your individual or organizational goals. I encourage you to seek out other resources and perspectives on each trait. But I do stand firm in my suggested progression and the need to develop a limited core of traits.

The eleven core character traits are broken into three categories. The initial traits are humility, caring, teamwork, and effort. The mental toughness traits are courage, discipline and perseverance. The excellence traits are initiative, commitment, leadership and awareness. Finally, the core traits are listed in the chronological order in which I suggest they should be acquired and strengthened.

The 11 Core Character Traits

The Four Initial Character Traits

1. Humility- To recognize room for improvement one must be humble enough to realize there is such room. Often times one must be humbled before they will embark on a quest to improve their character. Humility eliminates ignorance and allows for growth. Without humility a person or organization will see no room for improvement. What you might not realize is that before you can build yourself up, you must see how you are pulling yourself down.

2. Caring- To find a reason to reach goals one must learn to care about something or someone. This could be another person, a team, a cause, a goal. Caring about something or someone provides a catalyst for improvement. Caring eliminates apathy and accelerates improvement. Without caring a person or organization will have no reason to catalyze improvement or complete their tasks with maximum effort. If you don't care you will be the same as everyone else. A person who lacks pride will never have more than what another person or random good fortune has given them. Pride is simply a matter of caring or not caring. Caring is the initial spark which gets a person or group started towards separating themselves from everyone else. Caring gets you competing and forces you to pay attention. When we need to initially find our motivation, or rediscover it, what we are really looking for is a reason to care.

3. Teamwork- To achieve something one cannot achieve alone one must learn how to work with others towards a shared goal. This interaction allows one to practice selflessness and sacrifice. In return, one gains from the insights and abilities of others. A team could be any group at home, at work, in activities, or in sports. Teamwork helps to eliminates justification. Without teamwork improvement and performance will be limited.

4. Effort- To do the work required to reach goals one must learn how to work hard towards producing a product of excellence. Without effort the individual or team will not perform to potential. If you do not work hard your efforts will be limited and this will limit how much you can improve your performance. Effort gets you beyond your natural ability and allows you to distinguish yourself from others. A person or group will be stalked by their potential until they give it some attention and feed it hard work.

The Three Mental Toughness Traits

5. Courage- To reach challenging goals one must get beyond their fears and learn how to summon and maintain bravery. Without courage a person or organization will freeze or flee when encountering adversity. If you do not have courage you will be too afraid to attack an arduous task or compete against formidable foes. Courage gets you past your fear of doing what needs to be done.

6. Discipline- To overcome internal factors to consistently reaching goals one must learn how to maintain focus and manage their behavior. Discipline is vital in order to develop consistency. Discipline allows one to learn how to consistently start, continue, and stop their thoughts and actions. Without discipline effort will not be sustained or finalized. Discipline governs our choices between immediate gratification or delayed gratification.

7. Perseverance- To prevail over the external factors which dissuade us from reaching goals our goals one must learn how to overcome the inevitability of obstacles and adversity. Perseverance is the ability to go over, under, around or through those things that get in the way of a person or team achieving to their potential. Perseverance allows one to avoid quitting when faced with these challenges.

The Four Character Traits of Excellence

8.Commitment- To follow through on goals one must learn the depths of devoting themselves to the completion of a goal or cause through the commitment process. Commitment allows one to fully contribute to a cause and to finish what they have started.

9. Initiative- To recognize opportunities to reach goals one must learn to do things they see need to be done without being asked. Without initiative, an individual or organization will not seek out nor act on opportunities to improve. If people do not have initiative they will settle for less, often much less, than their potential.

10. Leadership- To help individuals and groups to reach goals one must be willing and able to inspire and guide others. Leadership helps the individual or group to navigate the twists & turns of decision making. Without leadership both large & small decisions remain unclear.

11. Awareness- To obtain the ability to recognize the myriad of variables involved in reaching challenging goals one must reach this; the highest level of character. Awareness requires a certain mastery of the other ten traits. When one becomes aware they recognize ingredients and connections which most others cannot see; near and far, large and small, past and present, internal and external. Every action or inaction has a short term cause and effect and a long term cause & effect. Awareness allows

one to see all of that & decide accordingly. Awareness allows one to see events and behaviors from a variety of perspectives, thus coming to a truer conclusion. Awareness allows one to make better informed decisions.

As you read about these traits in further detail in subsequent chapters think of something you are trying to make happen. This could be a goal or a project in sports, school, or career. Think of all the factors and ingredients which need to be available, surmounted, ignored, and executed in order to succeed in what you are trying to accomplish.

What role do character and mental toughness play in those things? I bet you say a big role. But I also bet you do little or nothing in regards to initially approaching the work you or your organization need to do from the perspective of the character and mental toughness of the people involved. Instead you likely talk about methods and strategies as you chart a path to your goal, but ignore these simple foundations of character and toughness.

If this foundation is weak projects will crumble. Even though it is a key ingredient many people don't even talk about character. I bet they don't even talk about mental toughness. It is very likely that if they do talk about them they only talk about them after the fact, after the damage is done. They will likely complain because character and mental toughness are missing, yet they have done little or nothing to promote them beforehand.

It is as if you are trying to cook a particular meal without the salt, sugar, butter, or flour that are important parts of the recipe. What ends up on your plate is unappetizing. Lack a character trait and you could end up with bland experiences. Fail to exclude a negative character trait and what you end up with could be distasteful or repulsive. If the preparation lacks mental toughness your achievement will end up undercooked. Likewise, it is important to understand the order in which the proper ingredients should be incorporated. Either way your banquet feast or casual dinner will not be nearly as good or as efficiently prepared as it could have had you consulted a cookbook or given the process ample forethought. Your favorite chef has an awareness of all the variables to a meal including the source of the ingredients, the final table presentation, and the character and mental toughness needed by the preparer along each step of the way.

The lack of strength in a particular trait will show up with some new step towards the goal or some new project. If the traits are poorly formed they will continuously show up with each new step and each new project. These weaknesses may be irrelevant to you in the moment, but bare them in mind when you or your team faces new difficulty. As you do, remember if you had taken the time at the beginning of the project or before the season to address these issues, you would likely not have to be addressing them at a pivotal moment of your project or season. Even if you do address these issues ahead of time and they do show up later, you have planted a seed which will allow you to address them more efficiently.

When you want to accomplish something, first ask yourself what role the core character traits will play in achieving that goal. For example, I will think through what my teams' needs will be before a game. If we are facing an opponent with large players, I know my own players will need to find courage as soon as they see these behemoths get off the bus. I know well beforehand I must address my team about their need for this particular character trait at that particular moment before the game.

We usually play our games on Friday nights. At the conclusion of our Thursday practice I will talk to our players about the hours that remain before the game and then the game itself. Strength in various character traits is needed as my players must eat the right things, get the appropriate amount of sleep, control their emotions in school the next day, and remember their equipment and the times we will meet. I will talk to them about the character traits needed from the minute they arrive at the field until the games starts. Of course, I will address the character traits we will need during the game and even after the game.

We can lose games because our players didn't hydrate or eat or sleep right. If they don't behave appropriately during school we could lose them for disciplinary reasons. If they get too amped up to play, too early in the day, they might show up fatigued come game time. We have had very good players show up to games missing a piece of their equipment. Even if we can find a replacement for what they are missing, that small event can distract the player and others from focusing on what they need to do before the game. Likewise, if a player shows up late or misses a pre-game meeting it can distract the entire team. Any of these issues can result in a poor performance and a loss. When my teams have strong character as a whole and understand how character plays a role in everything they do or don't do, we have as much success as our talent and good fortune will allow. In the end, that is all you can really hope for as a coach. Give some forethought to where in the process of achieving your goals each of the traits will need to present themselves.

If you and/or your organization address and master these core traits, then you will be better prepared to successfully pursue your specific endeavors and reach your goals. Until you do, your weakness in these areas will impede performance. If you doubt me then keep these traits in mind the next time you or your organization hit an impasse. Most problems individuals or organizations face can be traced back directly to an unaddressed weakness in one of these traits or an unplanned instance in which they will present. In short, these core traits are at the foundation of sustained success. The stronger this foundation, the more likely success will be achieved. The stronger this foundation, the easier it will be to identify and address problems as they arise.

Become aware of character and mental toughness and develop your vision through the use of a daily journal or a nightly reflection. Ask yourself some questions. What you did I do today that took character? How can I continue this? What did I see from someone else today that demonstrated character? What can I learn from this?

What did I do today that took mental toughness? How can I continue this? What did I see from someone else today that demonstrated mental toughness? What can I learn from this?

What did I do today that lacked character? How can I change that? What did I see from someone else today that showed a lack of character? How can I help them change this?

A big part of being a winner is being able to keep up with the winners. It's not about being positive or negative; it's about being real. Real perspective creates real change by real acceptance inspiring real action.

The base is wide & the peak is narrow. There are more people at the base than the top. The race isn't about getting to the top. The race is to see who can get better faster, and quite possibly to see how many peaks may be surmounted.

People and events are complex. But when one starts off with a firm foundation in The Character Way, one avoids all the time consuming missteps and missed opportunities continuously presented by The Easy Way. By taking The Character Way approach, one might start a little slower, but gain speed as they make better decisions on their journey to the target.

Ultimately, the person or group using The Character Way will achieve worthy objectives more quickly than those who rely on talent and whimsical fortune alone. More importantly, adoption of The Character Way mindset allows one to reach a broad range of goals and therefore to achieve a great deal more overall than those mired in The Easy Way of each new task. Instead of asking themselves what's The Easy Way to do something, those adopting The Character Way start by asking, "What's The Character Way to do this?"

This is the mindset that makes individuals and groups better. As one of my former players, Matt LeClair, who got the most out of his athletic abilities and has gone on to fine academic achievement, recently posted on a social media site, "The most important lesson in life I ever learned; if you have character and mental toughness everything else will fall in line." I have heard many of my former players and students repeat variances of this familiar phrase as they have gone on to do great things and come to recognize how many of their peers have accomplished little or less within the same time frame.

The mistake the narrowly accomplished and unaccomplished have made is in thinking character plays a small role in their life or organization.

The broad achievers realize every decision, every day, is character based. It takes some time and effort but if you stay on The Character Way you will recognize how much stronger you and the people you lead have become in comparison to those who take The Easy Way. As character is the fate of the individual so too is it the fate of a team, a school, a company a family or community.

"Let us not say, every man is the architect of his own fortune;
but let us say, every man is the architect of his own character."-George Boardman

Great natural talent will allow you or your organization to excel in one area. Strength in the initial character traits will allow you or your team to succeed in many areas until things get difficult. Once strength is built in the mental toughness traits these difficulties may be overcome. Finally, mastery of the traits of excellence will allow you to lead others to greatness in many areas.

In the end you don't need to be able to judge a person or group by the content of their character. All you have to do is patiently await the inevitable results. Investment in The Character Way can help you, and those you work with and lead, secure inevitably better results.

4

HUMILITY

*"Do you wish to rise? Begin by descending. You plan a tower that will pierce the clouds?
Lay first the foundation of humility."-Augustine*

"Humility, that low, sweet root, from which all virtues shoot." —Thomas More

There is no arguing with, nor teaching of, a narcissist. The narcissist
may be excellent in areas where they have great natural ability but they will
never be able to translate that success to all areas of their life. They think
they are great enough in front of the classroom, making the office cubicle
rounds or pulling out in front of us on the roadway. Common examples
are found daily in the sports page or on the celebrity shows as great players
and entertainers just can't seem to replicate the success they found in the
spotlight while in the shadows of their private lives.

A person who is humble realizes they have tremendous room for
growth. They realize there are so many people out there who are so much
more skilled and knowledgeable. People who are humble realize that, given
a bit of misfortune or different circumstances, they could very easily be
much worse off than they are today. People who are humble realize they
can always get better. They are aware of how much more they can still
learn and achieve.

Picking up this book, any book, is an act of humility. By opening the
pages you are tacitly implying you don't know everything and could learn a
thing or two. Your character is already evident and you are going to be
better because you are going to learn, at least a little something, and you are
going to learn because you are humble. The conceited and egotistical are in

jeopardy of proving themselves foolish. They seem to know only a small part of the world they live in. They are experts only in their own narrow perspective of the world.

As a coach, I often encounter young people who are not humble. Many times their parents fail to recognize this lack of humility or feel humility is important. These players have often had success at the youth level and think they are better than they are. This is not to say they lack natural ability. However, as they enter secondary school they find others catch them or pass them by. This is because players with humility realize they need to work on their game and train hard. The humble grow due to their character while the budding narcissistic youth stars are still largely dependent on their natural ability. Some youth stars have never had to develop their character because they formerly saw no need to work on their mental and physical skills due to their physical dominance.

These same types of occurrences happen during other periods of transition. For example, the dominant high school student or athlete who enters college and fails to see she is now competing against others of similar talent or the college grad who enters the workforce and fails to recognize the merits of those who have the advantages of decades of experience.

In my conversations and reading I often find humility seems to be a source of generational conflict. One of the difficulties older generations encounter when dealing with younger generations is the latter's apparent lack of humility. The young have come of age in an era where it was common for their parents to not allow them to make mistakes, self-inflicted or otherwise. Because this group has never been allowed to fail, they have seldom been humbled. Failure can be the most important catalyst of humility. The helicopter parent has sacrificed the invaluable lifelong lessons of humility at the altar of building unendurable self esteem. When real life hits such poor children the results are often a stubborn inability to recognize they have failed and stunning lack of means to deal with their failure.

The first time they are humbled can be traumatic. Sometimes this results in drama between the triad of parent, player and coach with the coach expecting player humility, while the player and parent expect automatic success. In these situations it is important to eliminate anger and frustration and try to resolve the conflict. Unfortunately, and ironically, a lack of humility by any or all of these parties can get in the way of such resolution.

"True wisdom comes to each of us when we realize how little we understand about life, ourselves, and the world around us." –Socrates

One of my most humbling experiences occurred within the first few days of showing up to college football practice. At a morning practice a few days into team activities, the head coach disgustedly threw his clipboard in my general direction. He did so because I was quite busy getting over powered when I wasn't heading in the wrong general direction. With the final toss, the coach told me I was to report to his office prior to the afternoon practice.

I went back to my dorm room and asked my senior All-American roommate if being targeted by clipboards and summoned to meetings was common place. He told me, "Guys get called to meetings, but Billy I have never seen anyone make coach throw his clipboard twice in a practice much less a single season."

On the way to the meeting I called my mother to prepare her to pick me up as I was about to get kicked off the team and lose my scholarship. She was the only person less pleased with me than the coach. When I sheepishly stepped into the football office the old man was sitting in a chair chatting with his secretary and puffing on a cigarette. When he didn't say anything to me, I modestly reminded him that he had wanted to speak with me. He turned to me and said "Billy, you don't know your plays and your bench press is anemic." That was it. He looked away and continued his chat with the secretary. I left his office and went straight to our strength coach.

I knew I was outclassed on the field, because I was outclassed in the weight room. My position coach and fellow freshmen had told me the same thing on a few occasions; all with the same disdain that had been expressed by the head coach. So I found myself a frequent visitor to the weight room between classes and practices. The place was every bit a dungeon; dark blue walls with a vast array of torture devices. Worst of all was the dungeon keeper; a strength coach named Dino. He was as wide as he was tall, and he seemed every bit the man that was assigned to torture those who found disfavor with his masters.

But there was something different about Dino that I instinctively picked up on. After a few weeks on campus I began to accept where I was and became oriented. My head stopped spinning and I learned my plays. It was around this time, when I was one of the few people in the weight room, that Dino pulled me aside. I don't remember his words. I vividly remember his message, and I remember it because of his tone.

He told me he knew I had never really lifted before. He said there was nothing we could do about that, but I would be amazed at how much I could improve if I followed his program. He didn't judge me on who I had been, but on who he thought I could be. No disdain. No vitriol. Because of his tone, I trusted him.

Yes I needed a "bad cop," a father figure of a head coach who wasn't afraid to cut past my justification and my feeling sorry for myself; a leader who was going to make clear in simple terms what was expected of me. I needed my peers to do the same. I needed someone at home who wouldn't allow me to run back to what was comfortable. But I also needed someone who could help me get past my previous mistakes and help me see who I could become. For a year I did exactly what Dino told me. The next Fall I started a few games, the remaining years I started all of them. My college football journey started once I had been humbled.

Organizations often have built in indoctrinations which serve to "break people down so they can build them back up." Their purpose is to instill a sense of humility which either consciously or subconsciously leaves the new member vulnerable and eager to find new ways to succeed. This occurs as the new member finds their previous knowledge or skill set will not be enough to allow them to thrive or even survive in their new environment. The organization and its seasoned members, often instinctively, recognize that if the new member is going to become a valued contributor she must first become willing to adopt the ways of the organization. Unfortunately, when these indoctrinations are combined with hostility and ignorance hazing occurs. This is obviously to be avoided and caution should be taken in a humbling situation.

"When I let go of what I am, I become what I might be." – Lao-tzu

Often humility results from an initial my way versus your way struggle between the new member and more experienced members of the group. As is human nature, the new member will seek the easiest path and expect the group to accept him as he is. When the new member is confronted with the fact that The Easy Way is not available, they will often quit and find an organization, activity, or occupation which requires less growth and adaptation.

In individual hand to hand combat movies a common theme is for the fighter to arrive at the step of a sage defeated and humbled. It is only through humility that the fighter will realize his shortcomings and realize he needs assistance. His humility opens the door for the teachings of the sensei. Humility makes one both welcoming of instruction and appreciative of guidance. Often times the learned will refrain from teaching someone who is arrogant or a braggart. It is the fighter's humility that makes the sage want to help his student.

"True knowledge exists in knowing that you know nothing." –Socrates

The first foundation of our football program is "Do what you are coached to do." Most of our players find this exceedingly difficult. They want to use their own methods. Because we work with adolescents a certain element of patience is required. Unfortunately, more often than not, a new player must fail using his method, sometimes multiple times, before he is humble enough to accept direction and put forth the required amount of effort and sacrifice needed to improve his performance. Players whom arrive in our program humble are more likely to have initial success. Simply put, they are ready to do their best at whatever is asked of them.

As coaches, we often talk to players about constantly getting better on and off the field. We reinforce this by breaking every team huddle by saying "Get Better!" In order to continue to improve, we must maintain our humility and we all need reminding. By telling ourselves "Get Better" we are also reminding ourselves of our mission in everything we do. If we stay humble and improve, success will take care of itself.

A person or team which is not humble cannot get better. This is because they think they already have everything mastered. They think they already have done enough to succeed. They think they already know all of the answers. Once someone has had some success, be it large or small, they frequently get satisfied, even a little lazy. They think the way they worked yesterday was good enough, so they struggle to work hard today. As a result, they stay still as the humble advance.

> *"Deep humility is a strong bulwark, and as we enter into it*
> *we find safety and true exaltation."*-John Woolman.

The only way to continuously get better is to continue to stay humble. There is a simple way to do this by tapping into natural competitiveness. Once you've beaten out the competition in your organization or community, envision the competition in nearby communities. Then envision the competition in the state etc. Then compete against those people every day. Not just in scheduled practice, but in study and training on your own. For example, you may be the best player, or teacher, or businessman in your town, but are you the best in your region? Are you the best in the state, the country, or in the history of those places? Are you out working your competitor down the street, in the next town or on the other side of the world?

How can a person determine if they are being humble? Well, a great way to see if you're staying humble is to see if you have had a case of the "too goods." Have you been too good to get to places on time, to do the grunt work, to help out the less experienced members of your group? Have you been too good to clean up after yourself, to study and train? Have you been too good to say please and thank you or to apologize? Have you been too good to be corrected or learn something new or to recognize areas where you can improve?

A person who is too good to learn from their current teacher will be too good to learn from an ancient teacher, much less an ancient carpenter, shepherd, or self-exiled prince. See, if you want to be great you stay humble. If you stay humble you always keep the mindset that you need to improve. If you keep the mindset that you need to improve, you keep working. If you keep working you keep getting better.

Like all of the core character traits, once you adopt humility it takes care of a lot of problems further down the line and in many areas of your life. Just remember, stay humble or stay still.

Here are some questions for reflection. Can you think of anyone who was humble or had a humbling experience? In your life, when have you been humbled? What were your reactions? How have you benefited from humility?

What might be the benefits of your finding further humility? What might be the benefits of someone you know finding further humility? How might you be able to help them in that regard?

"Without humility of heart all the other virtues are absolutely worthless."
—Angela of Foligno

5

CARING

"From caring comes courage"- Lao Tzu

The view that character and mental toughness levels can't be changed is even more ignorant and damaging than believing that they don't matter. Don't let anyone fool you. People can change their character for the better, but they have to want something bad enough to make the effort.

Countless parents have entered teacher conferences with me distraught about the progress of their children. In each instance, the first question I ask is if their child knows what profession he or she wants to pursue. In nearly every instance underperformers either do not have a future occupation in mind or they are struggling to tie their future ambitions to their current behaviors. My immediate advice to those parents is to help their kids figure out what they want to do or be patient enough for the children to figure it out. The parents always seem to leave a little less uptight and a bit more hopeful.

It's not that most underachievers are lazy; it's that they lack the vision of how much better they could be if they actually did the work. You likely think caring relates to treating others, your teammates, your students, your employees and clients, with kindness, empathy and respect. It does. But of equal importance is that we care about something. This something is crucial in life. Without it, effort is limited and as a result achievement is limited.

If someone does not have a destination firmly in mind then they are adrift. I want to arm my children with two things before they venture out to the vast seas of life. I want them to have a compass and a port. The port provides them with a destination. In a general sense, the compass I gift to my kids and players, or more often incessantly plead with them to take, is to become a person of character with the mental toughness to be counted on in any situation. Once they care about this, they make use of each day because it becomes their daily mission to row towards the ports of their choosing. They will learn to sail through turbulent seas and do whatever they must in order to get where they want to go in life. Finally, a little shove off in the right direction seems of importance, as any giddy empty nester can attest.

When you care, your actions have meaning because they are now tied to what you care about. If I care about my family having a nice place to live, I get up and go to work. If I care about my students getting a good education, I prepare my lessons. If I care about how I am going to look in the spring when I can no longer cover up with sweaters, I get on the treadmill.

A few years back I was on a ladder in the middle of January painting my house because I cared about cashing in on a government incentive to get the real estate market moving after the epic collapse. I cared because my younger children were reaching school age and I desperately wanted them to attend better schools. This program would provide us with a means to escape to a community with a fine tradition in education. But we would need to prep our house for sale and that meant painting in the middle of a New England winter. I cared so much I was out there freezing with a flashlight strapped on my head several times until three in the morning. My neighbors thought I was crazy. They still live there.

If you want someone to get on board, and start rowing once they do, you have to find a way to make them care and/or you have to find a way to tie what they care about to what you are trying to achieve.

Sometimes people talk about a teacher having "it." This is an innate ability to teach. The old saying is those who can do and those who can't teach. I challenge anyone holding that belief to stand before a bunch of disinterested fifteen years old at 7:30 AM and start talking about Federalist # 10. Before you start discussing political factions, you had better start the discussion by talking about social cliques and political issues under current debate in a two party system. In short, a big part of teachers having "it" is the ability of the teacher to make students care about the material they have to teach.

One of the most important lessons of World War II is the concept of appeasement. That's an easy and obvious opportunity to tie this major conflagration to bullies in school or the workplace. While many of my History students are interested in this event, I can make those who do not care pay attention by teaching them a lesson they can apply later in the day at lunch or in their after school job.

In my Global Studies class, many of my students could care less about developing nations until they realize the citizens of those nations are no longer content to ride bicycles and increasingly want to start driving cars. This change in economic status leads to an increase in the demand for gasoline and many a student is very concerned with scraping up money to fill their tank each week and take full advantage of the freedoms of driving.

Caring ignites passion. My players lift weights when they care about winning and making all-star teams and gaining the respect of the community. My players lift weights because they look up to their grandfather and want him to be proud of their performance. My players lift weights because they care about getting some scholarship money to help pay for college. My ever increasing challenge is to find out what they care about and then figure out how to tie that to their helping our team to succeed, and more importantly to their getting their school work done so they have more opportunities after graduation.

You never know what a high school kid cares about. They might want to get their name in the paper or a sticker for their helmet or to wear their game jersey to school so they might catch a girl's eye. The more a person cares, the more passionate they become about their efforts. If they really care about those things previously mentioned, no matter how obvious or seemingly frivolous, they will risk life and limb to go get it. If a young man can't stop thinking about that girl who only likes star football players, then he isn't going to skip any camps or training sessions and can be counted on to give his very best effort on a daily basis.

When we watch an athletic performance we are moved by a competitor who has great heart. Well what is heart? Heart is giving all you can for a cause. This cause could be a goal or a program, a group, a team, an event, or even another person. If you believe in something, and you have heart, you give more than others give; you give more than others can even imagine giving. That athlete is demonstrating heart because they care, and care very deeply about something or someone. Their caring has ignited their passion which has in turn led to their passionate performance.

You don't win when you can live with losing. If you can live with losing you won't do the work it takes to win. Emotion ignites effort. You have to make this workout, this game, this course, about something which gets you emotional. You have to make it so if you lose, you have disgraced the person you admire, or let down your little brother. You have to make it so if you don't get this done you're going to end up just like the person you despise. It doesn't matter if it's true; make it true in your mind. What matters is you get this game won, this project completed or make it to the finish line in a new personal record.

Picking up this book is an act of caring. I have no idea what it is you specifically care about. Maybe you want to make your character stronger, or you have a goal in mind you want to achieve. Maybe you want to get your students' test scores up, or make your employees more productive or win a couple more games each year. Either way, you have demonstrated you care about something or someone. Your character is already evident and you are going to be better because you are going to learn, and you are going to learn because you care. How deeply you care will determine how far you get in finishing this book.

People tell you to follow your dream for a reason. Without a vision of the joy of your accomplishment, you will never have the will to do the work to get there. Some aim no higher than the ground they now stand on. Some see no further than the walls now in front of them. When someone's vision is near sighted, opportunities become very limited. Some fish want to live in a little glass bowl and be fed. They never go far. Some want to swim the seas and hunt for their own dinner. They are likely to have a more educating and fulfilling experience in life, even if they have to go hungry sometimes. The dream pulls you along because you start to care about it. The journey to the dream makes you better than you would have been remaining completely content with your circumstances.

If something is important to you, you will find a way; if it's not, you will find an excuse. Impossible is an excuse. These sayings and their like are quite common. But what are excuses, except reasons not to care. So in order to make sure someone cares, and keeps caring, you have to help them eliminate their excuses. Some guys spend a lot of time getting psyched and motivated to get the work done. Some guys spend a lot of time thinking up a good excuse. You have to change their thinking. You have to make them aware of excuses, and the consequences of excuses. Once they have eliminated this habit of making excuses it creates room in their minds for finding motivation to get their work done. So as a pre-emptive strike I came up with some thoughts on excuses.

10 Thoughts on Excuses

1. Excuses are easy to find, people who don't make them or take them are rare. They have a name for these people who do not make or take excuses; winner.

2. The more character you have, the harder it becomes to find an excuse, much less make one.

3. Justifications are nothing more than excuses dressed up with plausibility.

4. More than anyone else, excuses impede the intended excused.

5. You can take an excuse from someone as easily as you can make one up on your own. People will be more than happy to offer one up to help keep you down.

6. You can make yourself a lot of money with justification, but you cannot make yourself a better person.

7. Recognizing the difference between a reason a person gives and an excuse they are making is best determined by identifying who benefits.

8. The fundamental component of mental toughness is in developing a mindset where you will not make nor accept an excuse for your lack of success.

9. The most difficult excuse in the world to resist is when a person justifies giving you something at someone else's expense.

10. The enemies of character are apathy, ignorance, and justification. One of these may usually be found at the core of an excuse.

You care about winning or helping someone else to win. But sometimes they have difficulty caring about why they need to win. Search for "why win?" on Google and you won't find much. In trying to motivate underachievers/low achievers in our various fields, our assumptions lead us to pass by the most fundamental question of all; why win? Winning teams are made up of team members who have found their own core reasons for winning. While some of these are shared, they are still individual in nature.

Michael Jordan was known to constantly look for reasons to win throughout his career. Some of his reasons were well known. Many were imagined or blown out of proportion. But he always found reasons to win and used them to compete at a consistently high level. In honor of the number he wore for the majority of his basketball career here is a list of twenty-three general reasons to win; to succeed at whatever you are trying to accomplish.

23 Reasons to Win

1. Hate losing
2. Keep momentum
3. Demonstrate improvement
4. Honor someone/ Show appreciation
5. Love (individual, teammate, organization, school, town, country etc.)
6. Disdain for someone (opponent, enemy)
7. Prove someone wrong
8. Be referred to as a winner
9. Gain Attention/Notice
10. Legitimize approach/philosophy/methods
11. Enjoy a Victory Celebration (Victory lap, Victory party, Dinner etc.)
12. Build Self-Esteem
13. Add to list of accomplishments
14. Make your sacrifice more meaningful and more worth the effort
15. Be remembered
16. Get an Adrenaline Rush/ Feel Good
17. Put a trophy on you shelf (on your wall, in your driveway, on your

finger etc.)
18. So others can win with you (win-win, carry a team)
19. Keep the streak alive
20. Revenge
21. Establish dominance
22. Permanence of Victory
23. Pride

Maybe pride is nothing more than the ability to access any or all of these reasons when called upon. Maybe a lack of pride is simply an inability to find a reason to win. Losers occasionally think about winning but winners never forget about losing. Where there is care, there will be sacrifice, and when you want to be great, sacrifices are a common occurrence. A locker room pre-game speech only gets someone to care for a few minutes; but it is the speech you give yourself and repeat to yourself which truly endures. You have to remind yourself what you care about on a daily basis.

Is there really anyone anywhere who does not perform at a higher level with a chip on their shoulder? One of the reasons teams from our school tend to start slow is they are not slighted very much. They live in a pretty isolated community and rarely interact with the kids they compete against from other communities. Our kids are not terribly sophisticated, so they miss the subtle slights and digs from the local media. So I am always trying to convey to them all of these potential slights. I help them find chips. I must confess, I have what my friend calls Irish Alzheimer's; you forget everything except your grudges. If you don't have a chip, find one or make one up! Just find something to care about and tie it to your goals. This finding of chips inspired me to write this little poem.

make no mistake be I younger or older,
comes time my dreams die unless I grow bolder
forge in my eyes the fierce stare of the soldier
strive to prepare not for pebbles but boulders
I rise to relentless once I find my own chips to shoulder

Caring also means a person shows concern for others by treating them with kindness, compassion, generosity, consideration and a forgiving spirit. It means being invested in the outcome of a cause or status of a group or individual. Rarely can a person make such a huge difference with such little effort. You can let someone know you care by doing the simplest things. However, if you don't care this also will become obvious. We are constantly showing whether we care or not by the choices we make and the actions we take. Although they may not be obvious to us, they are certainly

41

obvious to other people. Sure it is important to care about the people in your life. Likewise it is important to care about your fellow man, and the generations which will follow. When you care about them you will help them to achieve and they will help you do the same.

Do you arrive on time? We had a guy who was always late; late to class, late to practice etc. I confronted him dozens of times to be on time. I told him being on time shows other people you care. I told him it's easy to be late. Anyone can be late, but it's hard to be on time. It takes some effort. It's funny because he would always complain when his parents were late picking him up after practice. When this happened he would feel like his parents didn't care. I used to just shake my head. How can this guy be hurt when his parents are late to pick him up, but could care less about his teammates and classmates who hustled to class or practice and then watched him stroll in late? Will you have to learn the hard way? Be late for the bus to an away game and we will leave without you. Send in your college application late, and you are telling the college you do not care. They are not going to admit you. Be late to a job interview and someone else will be getting the job. Be late for work and you are not going to get promoted and may lose your job. Like most aspects of character, you have to work on being punctual. You have to get into good habits and be consistent. People with character tend to arrive early. They do more than enough to be on time.

Who you follow might give you a good idea where you're heading. What you give your attention to determines what you become. What you spend your time on is what you care about. But is what you are spending your time on making you any better? Is what you are spending your time on getting you any closer to your goals?

I spend very little time complaining. It doesn't help. I know very little about the lives of celebrities. I don't care about what they do, because it doesn't help me get where I want to go. I don't listen to the sports critics on television or radio. Their opinions don't hold any value for me. I care about getting better. I care about helping others to get better. So I spend my time on that. I follow the people who are going to help me get that done. A big part of the Character Way is recognizing what you care about and how that relates to what you are spending your time on.

Are you courteous? Please and thank you go a long way! When you interrupt someone do you say excuse me? Are you holding the door open for someone? Are you helping to carry in and put away groceries? Are you cursing in the hallways? Are you taking the lavatory pass for half a class period while one of your classmates needs to go to the lavatory? Do you pick up after yourself at lunch or at home?

Courteous people have an edge because they are showing they care for others and those others will most often care in return. Discourteous people show they care only for themselves and people then care less for them. A daily example occurs in our copy room at school. The lady who works in this room is a terribly nice person named Mrs. Shultz. She will go to great lengths to make sure my copies are done in time for class or practice. I can't help but feel this is due in part because I am courteous to her. I know she has a difficult position serving a hundred teachers and well over a thousand students. When I am in her copy room student after student comes in and the first words out of their mouths are "I need." No good morning or please may I have? Unfortunately there are a couple of teachers who sound much like those kids. All I'm saying is my copies get done on time and are accompanied by a good word and a smile. Heck they even get delivered most of the time; thank you Mrs. Shultz.

Looking someone in the eye when they speak shows you care. So does having your head up when a coach is addressing the team or your teacher is putting notes on the board. Caring could also be asking questions about whether a classmate got the job or won the game, or if someone is feeling better if they have been going through a rough spell.

Do you have to be told things more than once because you were not paying attention? Paying attention is often the best way to get better. In watching my son's play sports I am always amazed at how much better the kids who pay attention get in comparison to the kids who don't pay attention.

Bringing your notebook to class shows you care. Same as having all of your equipment for practice, having your physical by the start of the season, being in great shape for the first practice, participating in off-season lifting, 7 on 7 and camps etc. How hard you prepare is dependent on how much you care. It's difficult to look someone in the eye and tell them you care when you have not worked hard.

Finally your attitude is a dependant on your caring. Once you care about the outcome of your situation you will begin to care about your attitude. A poor attitude by a player or student or employee is just a reflection of a lack of caring. Caring controls attitude. If you want a person's attitude to change, then you have to find a way to get this individual to care.

I tell our players, we want you to be yourself, to be who you are. You don't need to be like everyone else on the team. But we do want you to be your best self. Have the best character you can, be as mentally tough as you can be. Find your best self and give that to the team each day. We all have to care about those things if we want to be successful.

I understand my players can only care so much about a game. I explain to them if we did all of these difficult things just for football, it would be a waste. Football does not last forever; we all have a last game at some point. They need to spend an incredible amount of time lifting, running and attending camps. But kids and their parents have a tough time caring about running and lifting and going to camp. That's a tremendous year round commitment of time and sacrifice. I tell them flat out such effort is too much for eleven games. But it's not about that. It's about the man you become. I care about the man they will become, they care about the man they will become and most assuredly so do their parents. That's what makes it worth all this time and effort. I tell them they must read, run, lift, talk, watch videos, go to camps, practice, etc. to be good at football, but also do those things knowing they will pay off in almost everything they do the rest of their lives. If they don't believe me, I tell them to just look what has already become of some of the guys who gave football up, and think about what they could have become had they stuck it out. I care about winning games and winning championships, but in the end what I care most about is my players being good fathers, workers, and citizens. In the end my trophies are people.

For some, the team, the sport, the job, or the project is all they have. As a result they care deeply and put forth a tremendous amount of their time and energy in devotion to that cause. You may not care quite as much or care much more about other things. There is nothing wrong with this, but you have to have respect for those who do care a great deal. You have to care about them and honor their effort by giving them all the effort you can.

In coaching two sports, football and lacrosse, there is always a struggle between those who are more devoted to one or the other but participate in both. My challenge as a coach is to get them to understand and accept this. I try to show them that the football players might not spend as much time on lacrosse as the lacrosse devotees would like, but the football players spend a great deal of time on toughness and can bring that to the lacrosse team. Likewise, the lacrosse players may not lift weights as much as the football devotees like, but they bring a great deal of athleticism to the football team. When you play two sports, you have to care about the one which is in season. It must become your priority in honor of the commitment of the in season sport's devotees.

Some people talk about "finding their why," but this is really just another way of finding something to care about. In helping others to find out why something I must teach or coach will be important to them I tend to think of the nozzle of my garden hose. The nozzle has different settings labeled as spray, stream, jet, or drench.

Most frequently, I spray reasons to care. In spraying I try to reach a broad range of people by reminding them of common reasons to care. At the start of a course I spray grades as they relate to college admission and graduation requirements. At the start of football season I will spray our long tradition and the necessity to continue it.

Throughout the season I will stream care. I will discuss a concept by relating how it comes up in class, sports and life. This answers why the group before me should care about a particular drill or reading assignment.

Sometimes I have to jet or drench care. I jet in order break through an individual's overall total lack of care. I drench to remind the forgetful or easily distracted why they must care. In the end, I know a class or team or community needs to be well moistened with care in order to start to change and continue to grow.

Can you think of anyone who was driven to great effort because they suddenly found something or someone to care about? In your life, how has caring spurred you to action or inaction? How has what you have cared about changed over time? How have those changes changed your actions?

What might be the benefits of your finding something new to care about? What might be the benefits of someone you know finding something or someone new to care about? How can you help them find a reason to care?

"No act of kindness, however small, is ever wasted"-Aesop

6
TEAMWORK

Team is a term we use, far too often, to describe a group of people in the same office, on the same job site, or wearing the same uniform. But that assemblage is just a group of people working on the same project. They will not be successful until they can commit to giving each other their best character and mental toughness. True teamwork is so valuable and sought after because it manifests as the power of character; combined.

In teaching The Character Way we always start with caring and humility. Without caring for other people and the ability to stay humble, a person will simply do things for selfish reasons. Selfishness is quite the opposite of teamwork. A person without caring and humility is just out for themselves. Once people develop their caring and humility enough, they can work as a team, but not before then.

The best teams I have coached and played on have been a true brotherhood. This is another term that gets kicked around too often. The misconception is teammates reaching brotherhood status have to like each other, but this is not true.

What sets brotherhood apart is caring and accountability. Just as you may hold a bit of disdain for your siblings; you may hold the same for your teammates. Likewise, you will not be accepting of anyone being brutally honest and forceful with your little brother; except you. It is your job to watch over him and call him out when he is being an idiot or a lazy bum. So to it is your job to find and expose his every weakness so he can recognize it and find strength in those areas before they are discovered and exploited by the outside world. In short brothers care about each other and keep one another humble. As a result they make each other better.

I am an only child so I learned about the brotherhood aspect of teamwork through sports. It is in those experiences I learned we may be on the same team, but if you can't keep up with your teammate or get on him to do better, or handle him telling you to pick it up, then you may be teammates but you are not brothers

I always considered myself a good teammate. I had the humility to put aside my own selfish interests in order to set about the tasks required for team success. I wanted to be a quarterback. I played the line because that's what our team needed. I wanted to play point guard. I played power forward because my team needed me to rebound and defend the post.

Later in life, I discovered I was being a bad teammate to my wife. I knew all of the traits of teamwork, but I didn't apply them to my marriage. Once I realized this, I was a much better husband. I took on roles I really had no interest in because I needed to assume those roles for the good of the team at home.

In coaching, I found myself talking to player after player about their selfish behavior. I used to get frustrated. But I eventually came to realize these kids had never been taught teamwork and what it means to be a good teammate. Now I teach teamwork and potential teamwork issues before they come up during the season.

The same holds true for my classes. I may teach three sections of a course but the collective class average grade in each section may vary wildly. Some of this is due to natural ability, but much is also due to the collective character and mental toughness of those kids sitting in those desks. I try to teach my classes that their grades are dependent on everyone in the room. If one of them becomes a grade anchor and starts talking incessantly about something unrelated to class, they will rope others into the conversation as either active or passive participants. This behavior will distract everyone in the room from completing their assignments and pull their grades down. Rather than constantly confronting the grade anchors, I cultivate an environment where there is peer pressure to stay on task. Most of those classes understand that if one person is off task, all of their grades will be lower because they will be unable to pay attention to the material or complete their assignments. The message is simply being a good classmate is important to everyone.

Sometimes it helps to identify the actions of a good teammate and compare them with the opposing qualities and behaviors of a bad teammate. By making my players aware of this before the season starts, they learn what is expected of them when they work together.

Good Teammate or Bad Teammate?

A good teammate is pushing himself so you can see how much you can push yourself. A bad teammate only thinks about himself and his own struggle.

A good teammate sucks up as much hurt as he can, so his teammates can benefit from his presence. A bad teammate can't get past the pain because he doesn't care about anyone other than him.

A good teammate shows he appreciates your efforts by giving his very best effort. A bad teammate is trying to get by with as little effort as possible.

A good teammate watches your repetition, and coaches you while your in line waiting for your next rep. A bad teammate is only hoping he won't have many more reps left before the drill ends.

A good teammate is not as concerned about you messing up as much as he is concerned with your fixing the problem. A bad teammate can't get past your mistake.

A good teammate isn't afraid of doing more than his share. A bad teammate spends a lot of time worrying about what his share is.

A good teammate is there. A bad teammate is somewhere else.

A good teammate let's you know he appreciates your efforts. A bad teammate is focused only on his own effort.

A good teammate gives you his best when you face him in a drill. A bad teammate tries to get you to agree to not go too hard.

A good teammate has good character because he works on it. A bad teammate has little character because he ignores it.

A good teammate is mentally tough. A bad teammate seeks comfort, ease, and convenience.

A good teammate can be counted on in any situation. A bad teammate can be counted on only when things are easy and convenient..

A good teammate looks for ways to win. A bad teammate looks for ways to avoid the work.

Worry about your teammates and you will discover things get easier for you. In the end your teammates are most concerned with your presence. Are you training, winning and even losing next to them? That takes care of teammates, but what about teamwork? Just as I try to define what a good teammate is prior to our season, I also try to give them examples of teamwork they will need to master through the course of the season. This alleviates a lot of frustration and confrontation.

Teamwork is...

1. having a common goal or sharing the same dream.
2. having a common identity.
3. not wanting to let your teammates down.
4. growing together when circumstances try to pull you apart.
5. trying to get better every day so everyday gets better.

6. sacrificing for one another .
7. is sharing the same work and responsibilities.
8. swapping turns doing the unpleasant so nobody always gets stuck with it.
9. sharing the burden or blame so you can share the glory.
10. doing your share, and more than your share when called upon.
11. asking for help when you need it.
12. helping out before you need to be asked.
13. what you do on and off the field represents your team .
14. helping one another to do right on and off the field.
15. motivating one another.
16. pushing one another to get better in the weight room and running together.
17. going to camps together.
18. the realization that teammates are sacrificing their time and effort for you.
19. having some fun while getting things done.
20. helping one another stay focused.
21. pointing out weaknesses to each other before our opponent finds them.
22. listening when a teammate is trying to help you out.
23. accepting criticism but not excuses.
24. forgiving yesterdays wrong while working for tomorrow's achievement.
25. knowing when to talk and knowing when to be quiet.
26. accepting you will not always be able to do as you choose.
27. accepting a bigger or smaller role for the good of the team.
28. when you need to follow and knowing when to lead.
29. using skills that complement one another.
30. feeling individual emotions as a group.
31. the reason for individual success.
32. the power of character; combined.

What are the differences between being a good teammate and a bad teammate in your sport, or classroom or office, or home or community? What are the instances when teamwork will be necessary to the tasks that needed to be completed in those environments? Will you identify these beforehand or will you continue to only address them as they come up during your ventures? Will you assume everyone is aware of what is expected or will you make sure everyone understands how their actions and inactions have consequences for the people whom work side by side with them?

Will you foster a sense of brotherhood or will you settle for just having a bunch of people wearing the same uniform or sharing the same space? Can you identify the individuals who will bring down overall performance and identify ways to use peer pressure to prevent that from happening?

7

EFFORT

"You can't cross the sea merely by standing and staring at the water."
- Rabindranath Tagore

When I first started coaching, I rarely had to coach effort. The same holds true for the other traits. That has changed, and I would find it very hard to believe the same did not hold true on other courts and fields, in other classrooms and in any setting of commerce. If you want your organization to succeed, you are forced to coach effort along with the other traits. There is really no other way around it.

On a personal level, honestly ask how much of what you have has been given to you and how much has been earned by you. True pride cannot be given and must be earned. If we don't develop our character and mental toughness, then we will not do the work that needs to be done. Success will then elude us. Talent only gets you so far. We all reach a point where work is required to progress and develop to our potential. Character gets you working and mental toughness keeps you working no matter what. That's why they are key; if you have them you will unlock the barriers to getting the work done.

The achievement gap will only close once we learn to close the character and mental toughness gap. We have a growing number of people who have never been properly taught that each competitive instance presents a price to pay for success. If you haven't earned enough to cover that price, you can't buy the win. You can't put winning on a credit card. It has to be paid, in full, in advance. Talent and connections can get you places, but eventually you have to pay a cover charge of character and mental toughness galvanized effort to get into the success club at the next level.

This is what it's really all about. Without this infused effort the individual or group does not get better. They have to run the run, row the seas and build the buildings. But without character there will rarely be quality work. Without mental toughness work will be inconsistent. Wanting it isn't enough to get it. You have to find the character & mental toughness to do the difficult undertakings and keep doing the work no matter what.

It's not that you practice or prepare. Anyone decent will train. No it's about how you practice. How much energy and will do you bring to each training session and learning experience?

You can't expect to do average people things if you want to be better than average at what you do. If you want to be good you work hard all week. If you need to be good you get extra work in before or after practice or work. Watch training or motivational videos, get extra practice in when you are not asked to do so. Everybody trains and practices; it's doing that with character and mental toughness that gets you better than your competition. Your being the first one in and the last one out matters little if you are not exerting great effort while you're there. Anyone can punch the clock and find ways to dawdle.

Losers focus on the pain and inconvenience of the moment; winners know it will end and instead focus on the good that comes from what they must endure. Losers think a few training sessions won't matter. Winners have seen the results of their effort and know every single rep of a physical workout or page of a mental workout matters.

Compared to your neighbor you might seem an over-achiever, but your competition is rarely next door. Compare yourself to opponents both near and far. Who do you compete against each day? The bigger your competitive radius the more motivation you will have to hustle. Compete against those you don't see.

One of the things many have trouble realizing is that effort fuels fun. When we approach tasks with a looming sense of misery, we become lethargic and time slows down. When we truly work hard we are competitive and energetic and we are having fun. When we're lazy we are not competing nor having fun. It's that competition that makes it fun. The harder we work the more fun we'll have. This is a terribly difficult thing for people, particularly the young, to understand

Sometimes work is monotonous, but if you make it fun it becomes endurable. During his time playing football at Springfield College, John Cena and his teammates called their offensive line coach Reptilla or Coach Moore Reps. As they did their punishing drills rep after rep they exhibited the finest sense of humor. This was their way of not letting otherwise unpleasant work deflate them. They were great as a result the drudgery they pushed through. So much so that one year our team rushed for more yards than any team had in the history of college football. We won a lot of games and enjoyed the competition even when we lost. While John went on to become well recognized for his skills as an entertainer and his philanthropy with the Make A Wish organization, many others from that group have become great teachers, coaches, lawyers, medical professionals, and fathers. I have little doubt that they made the arduous humorous on their path to success and are having fun with the fruits of their labors.

Some kids fail to see the fruits of hard work. One year a big kid who was going to be a freshman and played another sport decided that he wanted to give football a shot. He showed up for one of our lifting sessions. He walked into the weight room and saw the size of a couple of our seniors. He made some comments to one of his friends saying that he wasn't as big as those kids so he wasn't going to play. What saddens me is the kid instantly failed to recognize that those seniors were big because they had put in four years worth of work in the weight room.

Kids seem to be taught that they are either naturally good or naturally bad at sports or school and they cannot improve. They seem unaware of the concept that hard work can make someone of average intelligence a salutatorian while a lack of effort can put a very intelligent student at the bottom of the class rankings. It's important from the start to make it real clear that hard work makes you better, and that a lack of it makes you worse as those who work harder pass by those who don't. This is why we always say are you getting by or getting better?

Paying dues is important. In our financial life we can put things on the credit card. This allows us to have what we want without feeling the immediate pain of paying for it. In our home life many a kid can have whatever he wants without feeling the pain of paying for it. At the youth level many a player has the natural size and athleticism to succeed without paying for that success in practice.

Well in high school you have to start pre-paying for success because things are no longer handed to you, and the competition is better. Therefore character becomes increasingly important. You want good grades so you can get into a college; you have to pay your dues by studying and completing assignments. You want to be a good player on a good team; you have to pay your dues in the weight room and in practice. This is very difficult for some to accept; not only the students and players, but also for some of their parents. They put their efforts into trying to find The Easy Way.

As a football coach, and teacher, I often have to be the bearer of bad news. I have to tell kids and their parents that if they want the student or athlete to be successful there is a very high cost for that success. It means a ton of time and some excruciatingly painful effort. I am very direct when I have these conversations.   I want to make sure people realize the ramifications of the decisions they are making. Unfortunately, I have been called mean for being kind enough to inform people that life can be mean. Fortunately, most people come to thank me for putting things in their proper perspective and helping them to understand that one's actions had better reflect their goals if they want to achieve something.   Delayed gratification is a tough thing to learn when you're young, but studying gets you in college, and weight lifting gets you in the game

We have a saying we use; block to the whistle. A football play starts at the snap and ends with a whistle. On a run play all of our players, except the ball carrier of course, are taught to block as hard as they can for the duration of the play. All offensive coaches always tell their players to do this. But our players actually do. You will see our players run 40 yards down field to block a player, or block a player and then get up to block another, or stay on their block for almost seven or eight full seconds. We have tried to instill a sense of relentlessness in our players.

Unfortunately, some officials and opponent fans in our area do not like this approach. They are offended by how hard we play. The opponent fans complain and call us dirty. I disagree; maybe they don't know the rules. What we have real trouble with are the officials who tell our players they are "blocking too hard" or "blocking away from the play." There are no such rules in the rule book. These officials simply disagree with our style of play. They believe our player should not block a player who is away from the play. But I disagree. We are simply trying to negate our opponents' hustle with our superior effort.

Too many times I have witnessed an opponent defender show tremendous effort and catch a ball carrier from behind. In fact as a high school defensive lineman I was awarded a college football scholarship largely because on multiple occasions I tackled a ball carrier who ran to the other side of the field. I caught those runners thirty to forty yards down field by relentlessly pursuing them; which saved touchdowns. I'm pretty sure those ball carriers, and their coaches, had wished their lineman had blocked me even though I was "away from the play." The point is that we play as hard as we can; within the rules, and we should expect that some people will not understand that relentlessness, or might even get offended by that type of effort. We tell our players the same will hold true later in life when you "work to the whistle", "provide to the whistle", "study to the whistle", "parent to the whistle" and "love to the whistle." When I'm at my best I "coach and teach to the whistle".

We also try to provide daily evaluation of effort. We keep score before each practice when we post a depth chart. This shows each player where he is in regards to getting on the field. It clarifies both role and hierarchy. Depth is posted for offense, defense, and each special team.

DEPTH CHANGES is written at the top. It is on the computer so names can easily be moved as people move down due to poor performance or move up due to great effort. I always find myself saying to our players "If you do not like the depth chart, change it with your effort, which takes character and mental toughness!"

When I went to my first college football practice I was the fifth team right tackle on the depth chart. There were four left tackles. What this means is I was last. I literally started at the bottom. A college football season, a college football career, is a war of attrition. I got better. I passed a couple of other guys. But there were others in front of me that were injured or partied too much and failed out of school. In the end I never even started a game at tackle. However, my efforts at tackle led to my being moved to play center or one of the two guard spots. I may have never been the best guard or center on my team, but I was always either the top center or one of the top two guards. My ability to play both of those latter positions allowed me to stay on the field when other guys passed me by. Things change. What should not change is the mental and physical effort you bring each day. Sometimes that effort pays off in ways that you cannot see in the moment nor anticipate developing in the future. This is what is meant when someone says work hard and good things will happen.

We tell our players that they are responsible for checking the depth chart before each practice. During games taking The Easy Way will result in their not coming on the field when they are supposed to, which means they skipped checking to see where their name is on the chart. Once the game comes their lack of effort will cost us a timeout, or penalty or worse. This makes it appear as though the coaches are disorganized, after they have put great effort into being organized. Our having to burn one of our timeouts may cost us later in the game. This is not a mistake they want to make as confrontation by their peers and coaches is assured.

Repetitions (reps) per minute is a way that we measure our effort and efficiency in practice. There is a limited amount of practice time. If our goal is to get better, then we are going to want to get as many reps in as we can before practice is over. That is why we hustle from one drill to another. That is why our players are told to think fast and move fast. Good players and good teams move quickly. That allows them to get more reps, which allows them greater improve. Bad teams and bad players take their time. They get less done. They get better slowly, if at all. That's why our players are constantly being talked to about their pace. They are told directly and assertively by their coaches and teammates because it gets them moving faster. If we said "please think about walking a bit faster to the next drill, if that is ok with you," we wouldn't be doing the player or the team any favors.

High school kids are always looking for ways to differentiate themselves. Often this is through rebellion. When I was in high school some of my classmates wore tie-dye clothing to indicate they were different. Soon, everyone wore tie-dyes. When I first started teaching students indicated rebellion by getting piercings. Soon everyone had piercings. The current generation gets tattoos. They all seem to want one to indicate their rebelliousness and to differentiate themselves. In each of these instances everyone rebelled the same way. In the end they were no different than their peers, they were just conforming to the rebellious style of the moment. One true way you can always differentiate yourself is to work harder than others. Do the work others are too afraid of or too lazy to do. Study longer, lift more frequently, read books others won't read, or run your laps in lane three instead of lane one.

Winners actively seek out information that will help them get where they want to go. They are starving for any new tip or perspective. When a winner takes the time to teach someone how to win that person either pays attention or does not. In the end it's that choice that makes someone who they are. In public one can tell if someone else was taught character; in private one can tell if they listened. This is an important form of effort.

Pay attention and learn all you can when someone talks about winning. You could maybe care less at the moment, but someday it will matter. Someday you are going to need a win. You are going to have to win a game to get in the playoffs; win a practice drill to beat someone out for the starting spot; win someone's heart lest you suffer your own broken; win against the other applicants for the job; win a battle against a disease or win against a deadline.

For some this book is their best chance, maybe their only chance, to learn how to win. This is because I've won. I know how to win and I'm willing to teach you. When someone talks about winning you had better stop what you are doing and pay attention. Not all winners like to tell you how to win because it means more competition for them. It means they aren't so special because anyone can learn The Character Way and then win. So, when a winner speaks lock it up and focus. Hit record because you don't want to miss any of it.

We have a problem. We think that a winning effort is somehow over the top. We think that just because we work hard enough to break a sweat, we deserve to win. When we don't win we start looking for reasons other than our own effort. We do this because we *think* we are giving a winning effort, but we are really not. We think the effort needed in order to win is too painful, too time consuming, too demanding. We can't imagine that winning takes such a huge sacrifice. We think it is way over the top to expect to have to do so much in order to win.

We think it's over the top for a lacrosse player to take almost every face off, run up and down the field with the first midfield, play great defense, leave guys in the dust on offense, be unselfish with the ball, never complain, play within the rules, lift weights without being told, encourage his teammates and do it all as a freshman and sophomore.

We think it's over the top for a football player to break his leg in October, hobble through basketball practices all winter, run the bases in the spring, and run hills all summer, in order to rise to a senior year where he sets the school record in the 40 yard dash, becomes MVP of a district championship team, a contributor to a playoff basketball team and a starter on a state finalist baseball team and do it all while getting grades that are worthy of Ivy League schools.

We think it's over the top for a football player to lead both his football and lacrosse teams in scoring his junior and senior years, while enrolling in eight classes even though we only have 7 periods in each school day.

We think it's over the top for a football player to break his leg in his first ever football game freshmen year, and work his way to a senior year where he becomes the MVP of a state final football team, a starter on a state champion hockey team and a starter in the state finals for the baseball team.

We think it's over the top for a football player to lose both his parents before he is sixteen, and yet captain both his football and basketball teams and earn an athletic scholarship to college.

We think it's over the top for a kid to lift summer mornings three times a week since before his freshmen year and then ride his bike back home fourteen miles with a nine-hundred foot change in elevation in order to become the first all state football player in school history.

We think it is over the top for a kid to start lifting weights the summer before his freshmen year, become a starter by his sophomore year, and do so well his junior year that even though he misses most of his senior season, his athletic and academic work earn him a spot at a service academy where he can get his degree without paying a nickel for it.

We think it's over the top for a kid who is less than 5' 8" to start at quarterback and lead his team to district finals in football, hockey, and baseball while being an excellent student, the editor of the school paper and have an NFL cheerleader for a girlfriend.

We think it's over the top for a kid to start at quarterback and lead his football and lacrosse teams to a combined 26-4 record, while being president of his class.

We think it's over the top for a kid to come out for football his junior year, lift weights every single day after school, and attend multiple summer camps, in order to eventually be invited to football camp at a Division I program, while being such a good student and citizen that he is offered a full ROTC scholarship.

We think it's over the top for a group of guys to lift three times a week, every week, even if they are playing other sports, in order to take their team to the state championship game as juniors and seniors.

Don't kid yourself. None of those things were over the top. They were just over the average. That's what winning is, setting yourself above the average through your effort. Being a champion is going even further and setting yourself over the top of even the winners. Most peoples' good effort is only average to them; their good effort seems impossible to most.

All of these things happened within six years of my high school coaching career. I share these stories with my new players because I want them to know what is possible. Because far too often your players, your students, your children and your employees have no concept of what is possible and settle for mediocrity as a result. You have to remind them constantly that a valiant effort is possible. That while most people put forth an average effort, that is precisely why most people find themselves average.

Why do some kids pass a test while others fail? I have a student teacher. He took over a couple of my classes. He did a great job. He knew his content. He varied his methods of instruction. He incorporated technology into his lessons. He appealed to the various learning styles. In short, he covered all the bases. After he gave his first test to a class of 20 students, I asked him why he thought some kids passed the test while others failed.

He said some of the students are very intelligent and pay attention. They got A's. Some of the students are not very intelligent in regards to the content area and did not study or pay attention. They failed the test. Most of the kids are in between. Of this middle group, the ones who studied and paid attention got B's. The ones who were inconsistent in studying and paying attention earned C's. The ones who seldom studied and paid attention received D's.

Here was a new teacher, but he had come to the same simple and obvious conclusions of every teacher before him. All of the buzzword generating fad programs in education make us lose sight of the obvious. Students who do the work fair better than those of the same ability who do not do the work. Regardless of socio-economic factors, and every other statistic or variable you could think to apply, this holds most true. So who does the work? Kids with strong character and mental toughness are the ones who do the work. You want a scientific study? Ask a teacher; any of them; all of them. Too narrow a universe? Broaden the study and survey managers, coaches, small business owners, personal trainers or military professionals. Ask them if people in their fields who do the work tend to have more success than those who do not.

One time in my teaching career I was confronted by an administrator and asked to explain why about a fifth of my students failed in one particular section of a course I taught. My answer was the lack of character and mental toughness of the students who had failed. I'm not so sure that went over too well. But did it make it less true? We spend a great deal of time and money on educational gimmicks that make it easier for students to learn. Maybe we should use those resources to develop the character and mental toughness of those we educate to generate from them a higher level of effort. Something about giving a man a fish versus teaching a man to fish comes to mind. Providing ferry service across every educational puddle just seems an expensive disservice to the student who will eventually have to find the effort to row his own way across the open seas of life.

I have coached many football, lacrosse and basketball seasons. The players who were talented and worked hard have done the best. The players who had little talent and poor work ethic have done the worst. Most were somewhere in between as they had average talent. The ones who did what they were coached to do, and worked hard, did well. The ones who were inconsistent in following instruction and applying their work ethic remained quite average. Those who seldom did what they were told and did not practice particularly hard were pretty bad. The same could be said of their teams as a whole.

On one occasion a former player came up to me following one of our teams playoff wins. He asked me why his team had not succeeded in making the playoffs. I told him his team did not have enough guys with character and mental toughness. Because of that, his team did not do all of the work we had asked them to do, while the playoff team had.

During lacrosse practice one day, I watched as our players had begun to do our daily warm-up routine in a lackadaisical manner. I blew the whistle and brought them over. I asked them why I was fat? They looked a little puzzled, and then one brazenly said because I eat too many donuts. We laughed. I then asked them how many programs were advertized for weight loss. They all chimed in offering up the multitude they had seen advertized for sale on television or in book stores. I then told them the answer to fat loss was pretty simple. Eat less. Exercise more. Neither of which will cost me a dime. I just need to do the work. If they want to succeed, they will have to do the work; nothing fancy. Do the work.

We have an innate tendency to make things more complicated and complex than they need to be. This is a result of our natural instinct to find efficient answers for our problems. But in doing so we often find ourselves victimized by this impulse as it distracts us from the simple solution. Develop the character to start doing the work and the mental toughness to continue the work consistently.

At the end of the school year our faculty members are required to assess each student's performance based on a three category rubric. The first words in these rubric categories, respectively, are consistently, usually, and rarely. These words are followed by statements regarding quality and performance. But, to me, those first words are extremely powerful in their simplicity. Being the coach I am, I could not help but apply those three words to our football team; in particular, to the effort in our off season training program in our weight room.

On average, about ten percent of our players lift consistently in the Spring . Another ten percent usually lift. The remaining eighty percent rarely lift weights. There is a direct correlation between weight lifting and football success; bigger, stronger, and faster defeats smaller, weaker, and slower. Our players are well aware of this undeniable fact of physics.

I have done my utmost to convince our players to lift year round. Our staff has worked hard to give our players an opportunity to succeed. We spend a lot of time educating our players about what it takes to be a winner on and off the field. We have coaches volunteer to open the weight room three days a week after school. Still, the vast majority of our players rarely lift. This is because they lack the character necessary to do the work usually. They lack the mental toughness necessary to do the work consistently.

Successful football requires a strong commitment by a large group of people. Football in our community will continue to be a struggle until those "rarely's" and "usually's" become "consistently's." Individually, one will not achieve their goals until they consistently put in the work needed to achieve them. Consistently,Usually ,Rarely; which one are you? What does that say about your commitment to individual and team goals?

If you truly want to succeed at football, school, citizenship, business, life etc. then you should be consistently reminding yourself of the word "consistently." If you strive for "consistently" you cannot help but build your character and mental toughness along the way. Consistency wins, consistently.

Think about what you want in the long term and you will find effort today. Think about what you want today and you will get your tail kicked in the long term, or even worse quit so you don't have to face the results of your lack of effort. Inconsistent effort leads to a great many "almosts." These occur when you fall just short of your goal. If you trace back the reason why you fell short you will find almost in your efforts along the way. In order to remind our players how important effort is I found myself writing and sharing this piece anytime they thought their efforts were enough, but I knew more would be required to reach success.

ALMOST
Almost made each practice
Almost made the block

Almost walked away before the trouble started
Almost made the sack
Almost scored a basket, a goal, or a touchdown
Almost caught the ball
Almost made the tackle
Almost won the game
Almost made the playoffs
Almost made All-State
Almost made the play
Almost summoned the enthusiasm
Almost had the grades
Almost got accepted
Almost got the job
Almost said thank you
Almost found the courage
Almost picked the right thing to eat
Almost made it there on time
Almost lifted
Almost paid attention
Almost finished
Almost ran another lap
Almost stayed eligible
Almost read it all
Almost got enough sleep
Almost had a winning record
Almost did another set
Almost went out of your way to help someone in need
Almost made the last cut
Almost got ready long before
Almost made the commitment
Almost realize the second chance was the last chance
Almost graduated
Almost made the sacrifice
Almost got better instead of got by
Almost kept his head
Almost made it through
Almost double checked
Almost didn't quit
Almost took the opportunity instead of the excuse
Almost didn't get in the car
Almost got the education so you could get the job you liked
Almost held on long enough
Almost took the next step

Almost did well for yourself so you could do well for others
Almost picked friends and partners with character
Almost made the right choice
Almost took the lesson to heart
More than enough, enough, almost enough
Guess which one the winner chose each day.

I don't know about your experience, but in mine most of my losses have been by a narrow margin and I don't just mean in sports. But whether the margin is large or small a loss is a loss. It makes a huge difference in whether we can consider ourselves successful or not. By giving more than enough we ensure we have done everything in our power to gain that narrow margin between success and failure. Unfortunately, most people just want to give enough and do enough. This is just getting by and the results of just getting by are often disappointment in narrowly missing our target. When you do more than enough, whether you win or lose, you still have a sense of peace and accomplishment. More importantly, you get in the habit of doing more than enough.

Each year it seems we have a player whose career ends abruptly due to injury. When that happens, the player feels a profound sense of loss. However, there is a tremendous opportunity to console those who have done more than enough. They understand that they have done all they can to be great and take solace in their efforts. This makes it easier on them, but tougher on me. When the kids with heart get their playing career cut short my eyes tear up.

Finally, I will tell you one more thing I tell my players when it comes to effort. I would imagine similarities exist to this sentiment in parenting, academics and in each profession.

I have had many guys who have played for me who come up to me after our games or drop me an email. Sometimes I run into them at the grocery store or the mall. Usually we don't have but a minute or two to chat. We catch up on what they are doing with school, or jobs or family. They ask about the team and maybe my kids. We always remember something we laughed about and still find funny no matter how many years have passed since they played. But before we part ways they ALWAYS tell me the same thing. They all use different words; saying it their own way, but they ALWAYS tell me the same thing. They all tell me they wish they could play again. But they say this for a reason that most don't understand.

Sure they miss their friends and the Friday Night Lights, the band, the cheerleaders and walking with a little swagger in school with their jersey on. But that's not why they say they wished they could play again. They say it because they now know the secret. The secret, had they known it back when they played ball, would have made them good if they were just fair, or great if they had been just good, or legendary if they had been great back in the day. Unfortunately, their playing days are done. So they will never be able to use that secret they now know.

You might be wondering what that secret is. You might think that if you could just know that secret, then you too could become a good player, a great player, a much better player than you are. Maybe you could become the kind of success where everyone knows your name, not only the kids in school, but the kids in other schools and their coaches too. Well, I think you are right. I think if you knew that secret you could become a much better player. So I will tell you the secret. I will tell you the secret that every guy who ever played this game wishes he knew back when he was playing. But before I tell you, you have to answer some questions for me.

How much are you willing to endure? How much pain can you manage to withstand in order to earn what you want? How much exhaustion and pain are you willing to endure in the weight room, running in the summer, grinding your way through practices and games? How much can you take before you give in?

As a football player you will have to choose when to give up on those things and decide when they are not worth the pain any longer. I guarantee you that decision time will come. That little voice will start chiming in that you need to give up, that this is too hard. It is the voice of The Easy Way. It tells you want you want to hear when you want to hear it.

Now back to the secret, the secret is this; this moment, this moment when you choose to stop giving it your best, it will be more important to you than you ever thought, because I swear this to you; and so will those old players; no matter how many moments of glory you achieve, how many plays you make, or times you get your name in the paper, or all star teams you get named to, it is the moment you gave it less than your best that you remember.

It is that moment, when you said, "I had enough, I can't hang on another second, I can't run another step, I can't get up another time."

It is that moment when you said you could no longer give your best. That moment, gentlemen, is the moment you will remember. This is because that is the moment more than any other that will define you.

Everyone who ever played this game realizes they could have been a little tougher than they thought; every player realizes that if they had been more mentally tough, they could have done better in that moment, they could have given their best far more often than they did. That far too often they listened to The Easy Way instead of The Character Way and became less than what they could have been as a result.

So now you know the secret that you can give your best effort way more than you think. You can hold on much longer before you let your effort drop off. I told you this secret for one simple reason. I love those guys just as much as I love you and I hate to see the pain in their eyes when they tell me they wished they could do it all over again, so that they could give their best more than they did, so that they could be tough enough to get through the pain longer than they did.

I'm telling you this because some day that will be you along the rope line, or at the mall with your kids, and no matter what happens I hope we'll talk for a bit, catch up a little, and have a good laugh. Before we go our separate ways I hope you can look me square in the eye and in your own words, in your own way, let me know that you appreciate knowing the secret because you truly gave it your best effort and you were as truly tough as you could possibly be. And you know as a result of knowing the secret, you became the best person, the best father, husband, landscaper, poet or businessman you could be. You learned that your losses will be more than just games or playing time or accolades. Your losses will be all the things you missed out on because you listened to The Easy Way instead of listening to me and others who have always been there encouraging you to take The Character Way.

Get in the get better habit. For the true winner, effort becomes about something more than success in a specific area. It means developing a mindset of constantly seeking improvement in all they do and understanding how this will help them get better in all that they want to do in the future. Winners are quick to improve. Winners win because they improve faster and more frequently than average people do. Teams are the same. When average people are busy being average, winners are getting a little better; all that little adds up to the difference between success and failure. Winners appreciate the magnitude of the seemingly small actions and inactions. To them every day matters, every rep matters, and not just their days and their reps but those of the other members of the group as well. That concept can be expanded to the point that we should all be concerned with the efforts of our fellow man. Doing small unimportant things the right way will lead you to doing large important things successfully.

I may seem like Captain Obvious, but I am always amazed by how little coaches and teachers focus on what truly differentiates those who succeed from those who don't. If we screen out for exceptional talent or intelligence, or a true lack of them, most of us are somewhere in between. Our character and mental toughness will determine how well we do because they will determine the frequency, intensity and duration of our efforts. So chase it, coach it, teach it, parent it, administrate it, friend it. If character and mental toughness are the most important determinants for success, than make them the most important things your charges do. In the end excuses and justifications do not matter. Either the work gets done or it does not. The Character Way helps us to avoid such distractions. It is what gets us to consistently do the work!

8
MENTAL TOUGHNESS

Before we even start this, can you define mental toughness? Mental toughness is (__)? If you are good at picking up definitions from context, you might be able to fill that blank in pretty easily. People seeking definitions or other information are often led to web pages by typing terms into a search engine such as Yahoo, Google, or Bing. The following are just a few of the phrases that people have typed into search engines, and as a result have been led to my blog on character and mental toughness.

How to teach kids mental toughness , teaching mental toughness to kids, how to instill humility in young adults, how do you teach toughness to your children, how to help son with mental toughness, how to teach kids metal toughness, teaching kids mental toughness, i never learned toughness, how to teaching mental toughness in kids, mental toughness test for kids, mental toughness for 10 year old, how to teach "toughness", how to make kids mentally tough, how to teach a child mental toughness, teach a child to become mentally tough, mental strength for children, teaching mental toughness to young adults, making your child mentally tough, how to teach toughness to kids, generation y toughness, making your kids mentally tough, how to create toughness in kids, teaching mental toughness children, how to teach child mental strength, mentally toughness children

A good parent will teach their son or daughter character, but few are those that demand mental toughness and give their child the strength to reach their potential. My point in sharing some of those search terms is that parents, teachers, coaches, and employers are beginning to realize that their charges have failed to learn mental toughness and are unable to reach their potential because of it. The lack of mental toughness is holding these people back. A person needs to know that if they don't toughen up they will only later realize all the things they missed because they could only take The Easy Way in far too many instances of their life. We recognize this and want to find a way to toughen them up not only because we need their toughness to complete what is necessary for our collective success, but even more so because we loathe seeing people do less than they are capable of.

I have long held that the fundamental reasons for a person's success are their talent, character and mental toughness. The last two can be controlled and improved. I think most good parents and professionals understand and value character. However, I think that group has struggled with how to articulate, approach, and attack a lack of mental toughness.

Long ago I got tired of complaining about how soft people were becoming. I am not a critic. I am an educator. As a football coach, I have dealt with this soft issue for a long time. Players who have been afraid to hit, afraid to work hard, afraid to endure heat or cold, who are uncomfortable with any type of correction that wasn't overly sugar-coated, etc. Similar issues also take place in my classroom. Heck, it's so bad we frequently have kids afraid to pick up a dropped piece of paper or throw out a water bottle they left on the other side of the field. After all laziness is often quite simply a fear of work.

Most people can eventually identify the problems. What they have trouble with are the solutions. I did too. But after years of trying to figure out what to do, I realized I simply have to teach mental toughness. If I don't, the first time a kid is too hot or too cold, or faced with hard work, or pain, or correction, or he doesn't start or play the position he wants, or doesn't make the all-star team, or has trouble managing his time, etc. the kid folds, the parent calls, and the drama starts.

Rather than deal with that routine again, I thought it best to teach kids how to be mentally tough. I just found you really can't coach football to kids without mental toughness, and it is even difficult to teach kids in a classroom who lack basic mental toughness. I spend a ridiculous amount of time doing this, but I don't have much choice if I want my players and students to be successful. Along the way I found that many parents, coaches, teachers, and even some business people were looking for ways to teach mental toughness. I was humbled when they told me how appreciative they were when they come across my web page or saw the results our coaching staff can achieve in working with their kids.

When kids (and adults) are mentally tough, they get their work done. No matter the difficulty. No matter the distractions. No matter the adversity. When they get their work done, they succeed. Of course, a person can remain soft and even do well, but they will never achieve to their potential. They will be limited as to what they can do. Anyone can play a video game, very few can play football. Anyone can write a short paper, very few can write a novel. In some places, this is ok. But it's not to me. I try to set the bar higher than average because the average lose too often and miss out on too much.

As we begin new school years, new sports seasons, and new projects, give some thought to the words I will share with you below. Why wait until the problems pop up? Isn't it better to prepare beforehand? I hope you share these words with your friends, your children, your students, your players etc. I think if you do they will appreciate your efforts in trying to help them get better and reach their potential. The idea is to share the lessons before they are needed.

Wikipedia offers a couple thousand words in their entry on mental toughness. My definition is a bit simple; mental toughness is the ability to maintain character when confronted with stress. Stress is often caused by physical or emotional pain, inconvenience, great challenges or adversity.

Mental toughness and character are intertwined, yet distinct. Rarely can I find a way to talk about one without at least indirectly mentioning the other. There are many fine people with good character. However, that character may not remain consistent when faced with challenging circumstances. So a person's character can vary wildly depending on their level of mental toughness. As people vary, so do our individual levels of mental toughness. Only the most mentally tough can manage to maintain their positive character under duress. Under easy circumstance, or for a period of short duration, most people will appear to have good character. This is really no different than a person putting on a front of good character to impress someone. Anyone can have good character when things are easy. However, once confronted with stress, real or imagined, some individuals continue to climb while others crumble.

The coach featured in the recent Oscar winning documentary film *Undefeated* is quoted as saying "football doesn't build character, it reveals it." This is a pretty common statement, but I believe it to be cursory and misleading. I see young people, and even some older ones, building their character each day. I think what that coach is actually trying to say is that football reveals your mental toughness. It reveals how much stress your core character traits can withstand. It reveals your mental toughness level, undeniably and without mercy. So it's not the character that is revealed, but the mental toughness level in maintaining the rest of your character that is revealed.

Before our first game of the season one of my fellow coaches and I tried to demonstrate mental toughness to our team. We gathered them in front of a small portable bleacher. I pulled out a stout candle. I banged it on the bleachers a few times with a solid thud. Then I asked the players "is this hard? Is this tough?" They all nodded in the affirmative. Then my fellow coach fired up a hand held blow torch. He took the torch to the candle and it rapidly melted into goo. I then pulled out a framing hammer.

I pounded it on the bleachers. I asked the players "Is this hard?" They now stopped nodding and responded with a loud "Yes coach!"

My fellow coach took the torch to the hammer, but the hammer kept it's character. I then asked them if they were just going to appear to be tough like the candle and then melt when things got heated during the game, or were they going to be like the hammer and keep their character under the intense flames of competition. We won.

I have seen a book out there that advertises 177 traits of mental toughness. That is a little too much for me to manage, much less utilize in teaching and coaching young people and advising their parents.

So here are my ten core principles of mental toughness I focus on when teaching my players, my students , my own children and the adults I come across who have a genuine interest in getting better:

Ten Core Principles of Mental Toughness

1. Tie Actions to Goals- Teach them how to tie all of their actions to all of their goals. The trick is to teach them how to stay focused on the goal, and progress toward the goal. They need to adopt a mindset where they constantly think about their goals when they make a decision, almost all of their decisions.

2. Visualize- Teach them visualization. This allows them to see both positive and negative outcomes of their actions by working backwards. Don't just visualize the happy outcome.

3. Handle it!- Teach them to handle adversity. I talk to them about what they will do when someone is unfair to them or when they are tired, or sick, or in pain, or when it's too hot, or too cold, or when they have much to accomplish in a short period of time or when they want to have fun but have work to do. Because so many people quit when they are faced with any of these things, people will have a huge advantage if they learn how to fight through them. Talk about these things ahead of time, so that once adversity comes, they can make the right decision and continue to progress toward their goal.

4. Start- Teach them how to start. Teach them how to get up and get going when they don't want to. Teach them to fake it until they make it. Put the game face on. Teach them how to adopt a mask of a positive and enthusiastic attitude and eventually they will have a game face on. Clap the hands, jump up and down etc. Teach them how to energize themselves and how to get pumped up. Sometimes you have to just get started and once you start your motivation will meet you. It isn't so bad once you get going. You see results when you keep going. You see huge results when you keep going hard.

5. Finish.- Teach them how to finish. We all try to get away with completing a task with minimal effort. We are wired to do that. Like many of our animal instincts, we do better when we overcome them. We have an innate desire to be efficient when it comes to work. However, we often do a poor job as result, because we focus on getting through the job instead of focusing on making sure the job is done right. Teach them how to finish their laps and not stop one foot short. Teach them how to make the meal and then do the dishes and then put them away. Teach them how to sit until their homework is done, and then have them check it to make sure it's done right. Teach them how to maintain their attention in class until the bell rings. Teach them how to maintain eye contact when people are talking to them and to maintain that contact until the conversation or lecture is done. Never let them quit.

6. Know the Enemies- . Teach them how to recognize the enemies of character. Let them know when you see instances of ignorance, or apathy or justification; especially justification. Teach them not to make an excuse or take an excuse. Give them an excuse to be lazy, and then point out how they took the excuse, rather than demonstrating the mental strength to not take the excuse. Lust of ease and comfort absolutely destroys mental toughness and begins to slowly erode ones character.

7. Avoid The Easy Way.- Teach them how not to seek comfort and ease in everything they do. Will making things easier on someone going to make them better? Is making sure someone is always comfortable going to make them better? Nobody ever reached their potential by taking it easy and being comfortable. People never want to hear that simple truth. Teach them to look for the difficult way and not the easy way. There are surely better examples, but take them to the track for a run. Watch as they run in lane one. Teach them how they actually lost, because they failed to be tough enough to run in lane two or six. Turn off the air conditioning for a day, just to let them know they can survive the heat. The most important thing my father ever said to me was no and he said it a lot, but it taught me to prioritize needs and earn what I got, which was rarely easy.

8. Adapt to change- Teach them that things are constantly changing and that the ability to adapt quickly will serve them well in life. I hesitate to tell someone to "get over it." Because leading someone to stop caring can be detrimental to their character. I think "accept it. Learn from it when you have time and move forward" is a better phrase as it does not excuse accountability. But I say "you're going to get over it sooner or later, so get over it now" a heck of a lot to those struggling with disappointments in relationships and sports.

9. Don't complain- Most complaining is simply the vocalization of mental weakness as people vent that things are not the way they hoped they would be. Be aware of verbal and non verbal forms of complaining. I tell

my players all I hear when someone is complaining is that they are not tough enough to deal with the fact that things are not what they had hoped for."

10. <u>Make the best of it-</u> Whatever situation you are in there is a way to persevere and get something out of it. Even if it's a better appreciation for what you have, or had in the past. One must be careful because the weak and the ignorant will use this as justification to settle for less than they should fight and work for.

By no means is what I write considered to be exhaustive or definitive. It just works for me in my situation. I encourage you to find specific examples from a variety of fields. The consistent quest to learn and grow will lead you to increase your mental toughness and that will allow you to keep your character when things get difficult.

Mental Toughness is simply the exhibition of character under pressure. That pressure could emanate from a seemingly endless number of sources; pressure to conquer your human nature to seek comfort, pressure of great competition, pressure of maintaining performance against poor competition, pressure of high expectations, pressure of pain, pressure of the wind, heat, cold, and rain of the elements, pressure of time management, pressure of the ignorant, pressure of the enlightened, pressure of the living, dead, and yet to be born, financial pressure, family pressure, self inflicted pressure and external pressure. Pressure creates mountains and valleys and rivers and tsunamis of adversity.

Pressure also generates powerful waves of fear. Fear can obstruct character. Fear evokes three responses. Fight, Flight or Freeze. The person experiencing fear can either flee by avoiding the pressure, freeze and do nothing or fight their way through it. While different responses are called for in different situations (freezing might be a good idea when faced with a T-Rex you can't out run and you are unlikely to defeat), there is only one response that is correct in sports. That is to fight. If you want to succeed you have to fight through the pressure. Much of life is the same.

It would have been easy for me to give up on my dream of becoming a teacher and high school coach. I graduated from college with a History degree, but I never had time to take education classes or student teach because of my football commitments. I learned of a graduate program where your education classes would get paid for in exchange for coaching football. That was perfect. But I couldn't get into the school due to my grades. I missed the minimum GPA by .05 and found out the hard way that graduate schools tend to not round up. I took additional classes over the course of two years and eventually they let me in. I wore them down, but once I was there I found out they didn't have a program to meet my specific needs. I sought faculty allies, fought hard, and together we created an academic pathway to get the certifications I needed in order to teach.

I fought with everything I had to remain in the lives of my eldest children when I divorced their mother. Sure I was fleeing her, but sometimes that's the best decision for you and others and one that requires the most mental toughness. It would have been easier in the short term to stay married, but in the long run it would not have been good for me or my children to stay in the marriage. I could have given up on my eldest sons when I no longer had the financial resources to prevent their mother from taking them three states away. But I fought and made the trips to see them at least once a month.

I continued that fight when they moved eight states away. I kept calling them and sent them daily texts. I made financial sacrifices to pay for airline tickets for them to come see me or for me to see them. I could have complained about the inequities of the situation, instead I fought. My efforts paid off when I found this message on Twitter: "@shanewmoore: Don't know where I would be without my dad @coachbillmoore." I had reached my goal, not in the specific path I had hoped, but I had achieved what I had set out to do at the start of the situation. I wanted to be a rock of stability in their lives and now my eldest son was old enough and had enough character to recognize the achievement. Had I not fled their mother I would have never been able to give them a modicum of stability in their lives. Had I not fought the day would have never come when it all seemed worthwhile. We all know popular tales of mental toughness, and many of you have your own tales to tell that make my battles seem easy.

Few people understand that you can overcome all of that obstruction, fear and adversity in their own lives. That means most people do not understand or even want to understand. That larger group of people will always try to feed you excuses as to why you can't overcome obstruction, fear and adversity either. Since we are taken care of at birth it is difficult for us to relinquish that comfort or understand why anyone would want to or should.

The truest way to ensure that you will have mental toughness is to strengthen your character. The stronger your character, the less likely it is to erode under pressure. In order to survive my pitfalls and reach my goals I recognized that my character had to change.

Another way to promote mental toughness is with forethought. By thinking through potential situations and how you will react to them, you stand a better chance to maintain your character, because you have anticipated what might erode it.

All week we remind our players what they will be facing on Friday night. We not only talk about our opponent, we talk about the standings and what the game means. As we get closer to the date, we will take the players through every step they will face from having to get their equipment together, to getting on the bus, to getting off the bus and warming up. We will talk about what is going on in school, in our community and at home that might make us forget our character. The confidence that comes from this type of preparation is really just a means of strengthening our character when we can anticipate distractions which will impede performance.

The next way to strengthen mental toughness is to practice it. As a coach I always try to put my teams and athletes under pressure in practice. I will usually pick twenty or so minutes out of a two hour practice and make our athletes particularly uncomfortable. I will raise my voice and become more forceful in my tone. I will place them in adverse situations. I will be unfair to them. I will call penalties on them I know they are not guilty of. I will get on them about every mistake they make. I will have our scout teams cheat and mock the starters to make them more uncomfortable. I will have them call the starters names (within reason). Some people may think that is cruel. Well, would it not be crueler to throw a kid into a Friday night situation where all of those things happen and he is unprepared for it?

All of this sounds a little sadistic. But it is pain with a purpose. These guys have to perform under pressure. They have to keep performing after they make mistakes. The opposition, the opposition's fans, the refs, the weather, the media, even their families can be unforgiving on Friday nights. They can say and do unfathomable things that can shake a player's character. By putting players through a bit of hell during the week, we are preparing them to face the inevitable. These guys are much more confident in their ability to handle injustice, intimidation, and ignorance, because they have already gone through it earlier. They will certainly face some of it in life. They are ready to have character in any situation.

Anyone can be great when there are no expectations and no adversity. The ill informed will believe in the validity of achievement under such ideal circumstances. But the beauty of sports is that it mimics life in providing ample amounts of both. These repetitions when the stakes seem high are invaluable when the stakes are truly high. Sheltering my players from unavoidable adversity is doing them no favor in regards to the game or life.

Like I tell my students in Government and History, there are bad things and bad people out there in the world. They may not understand why we need a military, but they only need look out the classroom doors to see that we need lockers. While we can wish things were easy and generous and soft, safe and uncomplicated, they are not always that way; at least not for long. Sometimes the only way to learn how to perform in a difficult situation is to allow ourselves some measure of difficulty. Becoming mentally tough is impossible unless we are allowed to learn to handle ourselves under pressure. When you can keep your character under pressure and are mentally tough enough to be counted on in any situation, you become someone special.

There are certainly times that a person should not be tough. There are times when human compassion and empathy take precedence over the need to exhibit toughness. Because football involves people, situations will occur within the context of the program when a player or coach must choose to not be tough. That being said, football and life in general require a great deal of toughness in order to succeed. The mental toughness required to succeed should never stray far from our minds as human nature will drive us to seek comfort and avoid situations calling for toughness.

Another way to look at mental toughness is to look at the antonyms of tough. In doing so, one recognizes that they have a choice. You can be tough or you can be the antonym of tough: pleasant, easy, weak, and tender. Think of that when you are preparing for intense competition or anticipate an upcoming situation where you must perform under immense pressure.

You're only as mentally tough as you are today. You have a choice. You can continue to settle and feel sluggish and apathetic, constantly seeking The Easy Way or you can summon the courage to get out of your comfort zone, remain disciplined when you experience some temporary discomfort and embrace the energy that comes with growth, with learning, with getting better each day, and persevere in becoming the person the world really needs you to become through The Character Way!

9

COURAGE

"You will never do anything in this world without courage.
It is the greatest quality of the mind next to honor." –Aristotle

Everyone starts off afraid. The people who get over it are the ones who do the work. It's the people who don't get their work done that are most afraid. When people are too afraid to leave their comfort zone & challenge their weaknesses, those weaknesses will remain. We are slow to change because we lack the perception to see the merits of improvement and summon the courage to voyage beyond what is convenient and cozy.

When a man, of whatever age, is ready to partake on a mission to achieve a goal, he often initially finds himself hesitant. One of the reasons for this is that those around him may not be ready to join him or support him. They might not be willing or able to take part in the mission at all. So the man finds himself not only having to find the courage to set forth on his journey, but also having to accept that he will have to leave behind those he cares about. I see this struggle in the young men I coach. A player sees what he might become, and is ready for his journey. But he also sees those friends around him who are unwilling or unprepared for the commitment such a task entails.

The choice is a difficult one. There come instances in a man's life where he must choose. He can stay loyal to those he is with, but he must then sacrifice his opportunity to fulfill his potential. His other choice being to sacrifice the time and bonds he shares with those around him in order to become all he is capable of becoming. This is an individual choice, but one must clearly see that either decision requires sacrifice. Like all things, one will gain and lose with every step in his journey.

"Crossing at a ford means, for example, crossing the sea at a strait, or crossing over a hundred miles of broad sea at a crossing place. I believe this "crossing at a ford" occurs often in a man's lifetime. It means setting sail even though your friends stay in place, knowing the route, knowing the soundness of your ship and the favour of the day. When all the conditions are met, and there is perhaps a favourable wind, or a tailwind, then set sail. If the wind changes within a few miles of your destination, you must row across the remaining distance without sail." – Musashi Miyamoto

I encourage you to act out of courage and not fear when faced with these moments. Be true to yourself and be aware of what you must sacrifice. Make your decision to stay or move forward knowing that it is your choice to make, and consult your heart and head above all others. There have been times in my life I have crossed the ford. Other times I chose to stay still. I can only offer that I found myself most fulfilled when I found courage in making those decisions. Likewise, when I set off and resolved to accept the resistance of wind and current and found the determination to row any distance required in reaching my intended destination.

You have to identify the things that get in the way of your finding courage. One such thing for the young may be their parents. It is a difficult thing for a young man, a freshman or sophomore to speak for himself. It takes courage, but it is something that the young man must do sooner or later. It's tragic when the parent of a senior sends me an email or leaves me a message about something the young man could have said for himself. It takes courage to speak. It takes courage to speak up and call out your teammates when they are not focused or working to potential. If you can't speak with a coach about when practices start, you are not going to have the courage to speak up when someone is slacking or something needs to get done in a key point of a key game.

When my eldest son was little, I saw a coach rip him and his team for their poor effort during a half time. Every bone in my body wanted to hop the fence and intervene. The coach was saying things that had no technical nor tactical value. In reality he was telling the boys to execute antiquated techniques that might get them injured. But I held off. I corrected the technique aspect with my son after the game had ended. But I also talked to my son about getting ripped by the coach and told him it takes a lot of courage to maintain eye contact with someone who is pissed at you and then give him a mean look back.

You probably have an idea what courage is. However, I think the highest level of courage is when you face your fears for the good of someone other than yourself. When I think of courage I immediately think of Medal of Honor winners; in particular, Randall Shughart and Gary Gordon. Watching from their own helicopter they saw hundreds of hostile militia converge on the wreckage of another American helicopter that had been shot down. Knowing that no immediate help was on the way, Gordon and Shughart showed initiative and repeatedly requested permission to be lowered onto the crash site, where pilot Micheal Durant lay alone and wounded. Finally, after their third request, they received permission and were inserted into the battle armed only with side arms and sniper rifles. Both men died defending Durant and were later awarded the Medal of Honor. Their story is told in the movie *Black Hawk Down*. Both men faced their fears for the good of someone else.

There are obvious instances of courage in sports and I have been fortunate to coach players who have personified this trait. They have played despite broken noses, hands or feet. They have played with torn ligaments. They have played the remainder of their season despite being injured to the point where they know they will require surgery as soon as the season is over. To see them hobble their way through practices and games because they don't want to let their teammates or coaches down is truly moving. Their efforts inspire those around them to perform at their fullest. Their efforts provide all of us with life lessons on what is possible.

I don't think people can truly show their courage until they face something difficult. By this I mean the kind of thing that can knock a person down or off-track for good. We have had a few young people in our program lose a parent or sometimes even two. I am amazed at how these young people beckon the courage to keep plugging away everyday to get where they need to go. A couple of them have had to hold down full time jobs, while going to school and being involved with sports; full time jobs; forty hours a week. They have to do this because they have to support themselves. Yet at the same time they find the will to keep up with schoolwork and even get involved in sports.

I have also had students and players who have been gravely ill. There have been kids who get up at 4 AM everyday so their parents can beat on their back and loosen up the junk that ravages their lungs. I have had kids who came home late at night from their most recent chemotherapy treatment in Boston or New York.

In recent years we had a player who needed a liver transplant. He missed a year of football due to complications with treatments and his myriad medical appointments. He finally was cleared to play by a doctor and competed with all his might. He practiced harder than anyone. I could have used him as an example, but I tried to honor his wishes. Football practices and games were an opportunity for him to forget about what he faced off the field. He could get lost in being just another kid trying to make his team better. He fought back at his disease with humor. He wouldn't allow his disease to defeat who he was.

These young people have a burden that would emotionally cripple most adults. Yet they refuse to give in. They fight to live their lives to the fullest and do so most of the time with a smile. Their daily acts of valor rarely get recognized. Each provides us with an example that we can be stronger than we think.

Courage is a decision a person makes. When faced with fear all animals, including humans, react the same way. A sudden boost of energy caused by fear allows you to confront an enemy, play dead or run for cover (Think about facing a bear in the woods). But the key factor here is that you decide which one it will be. In football there is really only one choice; fight. In academics there is really only one choice; fight.

I tell my players they have to face fear in life. In school when you have a major research paper to write how do you react? Do you fight and get the paper done? In the café when you see someone being picked on what do you do? Do you summon the courage and tell the bully to knock it off? In practice when you see someone dogging it what do you do? Do you tell the guy who is being lazy to pick it up? Do you fight and do the best you can? Do you avoid dealing with the situation and look the other way? Or do you freeze under pressure and do nothing? When you have a big game do you run away and avoid playing? Do you freeze and play poorly, if at all? Or do you stand up to the challenge and fight with everything you have?

Every couple of years I made it a point to teach our players' courage by scheduling a formidable opponent from outside of our area. One year we were offered a chance to play one of the top programs in the country. Prior to the season I had a sign up meeting and I was pleased by the fifty or so guys who showed up. I gave all the players a copy of Doug Rigg's recruiting biography. He was a monster running back from Bergen Catholic who was getting recruited by major colleges. I then asked all of them who was going to tackle him when we played him that September. Only four players raised their hands. Our players clearly needed a lesson on courage.

We have played two other far superior teams like that since I have been here. The first time our players showed up with the fire of courage in their eyes. We played great and almost knocked off the number two team in our state. The second time we played we showed up looking worried and scared. We played awful. In the first instance our players had faced their fears well before the game. They fought their fear the night before. In the second instance, our players froze or fled from their fear in the days before the game. When they reached the field and finally had to see firsthand what they were dealing with, they froze again. When you know your courage is going to be tested, you had better deal with it prior to the moment it is needed. You had better start thinking about and working on your courage long before.

The beauty of football is there is no place to hide on a football field. Your courage, or lack of it, will be revealed. As in life, nobody believes anyone else has courage until they see it. In football you have to prove it over, and over, and over again. But that's a tremendous part of the fun. When you think you can't find courage, yet you do; that is where you will find your best self; that is where you will find your true confidence.

I am forever trying to get our players to lift weights and trying to get new players to come out for our team. But in order to do so they have to get beyond a great many of their fears. In one of my offseason notes to my team I put a picture of a door at the top of the page and then wrote about it's significance.

The most important door in our school is not the front door. Anyone can enter the front door and some might jest that little of consequence happens when one does. No the most important door to our school is the weight room door. It's so important that there is actually a cover charge you have to pay to get in this door. The cover charge is paid in courage.

This door makes people afraid. People need courage to overcome fear and get through this door. Those inside found that courage. This door separates those who found courage and those who have not. Why the fear?

On the other side of the door are strong people who are getting stronger. Being around the strong makes people see how weak they really are in comparison and that makes them uncomfortable. So, the strong get stronger inside, and the weak get weaker if they can't find the courage to come through that door.

On the other side of this door are people working for success. Many people wait around and hope success finds them, or hope they will just magically be successful. The lesson inside that door is obvious; you get what you work for. To enter is to force one to accept this.

On the other side of this door you have to learn techniques and rules. Many people are afraid to learn new things, because this takes them out of their comfort zone. When one must learn new rules and techniques they have to question the ones they have previously accepted.

On the other side of this door is aggression. Many people fear aggression, but football is an aggressive sport, and learning how to properly deal with your own aggression and the aggression of others is an important lesson found behind this door.

On the other side of this door is struggle. Lifting is a struggle. People don't see struggle as a price you pay to get better. Behind this door you learn how to struggle, and you start to see the benefits of struggle as you get stronger. On the other side of this door you have to pick up and clean up after yourself. Many people think they are too good for such things, or were never taught these things.

Inside this door you learn to be responsible for the benefit of yourself and others. You may be called to spot people, putting their safety in your hands. You will be required to rack your weights so that others may easily start when their turn to use an apparatus comes.

On the other side of this door is respect from the people inside. Most people will never realize the huge amount of respect you get just for going inside and working hard. Everyone starts off weak. Respect comes from demonstrating strength, but more importantly from demonstrating your desire to work to get strong. The people inside know how true this is because they earned such respect.

On the other side of this door it doesn't matter what kind of car you drive, what part of town your house is in, and who you are related to. Inside is a great opportunity to prove yourself on your own merits. Nobody starts off in their on third base. Nobody can hand you strength, you have to earn it on your own.

On the other side of this door you get called out by your peers if you are slacking. Inside you learn to accept others pushing you to get better and learn how to push others to do the same.

On the other side of this door is the man of physical and mental strength you can become. Most people fear trying to be their best, because they might fail. The people inside this door know what it's like to try to lift something they can't and they learn to keep trying until they can.

On the other side of this door are laughs and jokes, bonding and brotherhood, and a sense of pride. Most people would never imagine such fun is behind this door.

A simple door, but to open it and step inside is to confront one's fear of all their weaknesses in all of the character traits. What are the thresholds that you are afraid to cross? Will you be better for crossing them? What fears have you faced in your journey from which you can fuel your confidence? What fears are those around you facing that you might not be aware of?

10

DISCIPLINE

"To discipline one's habits and efforts and wishes, to organize one's life and distribute one's time, to measure one's duties and assert one's rights, to put one's capital and resources, one's talents and opportunities to profit: again and always order. Order is light, peace, inner freedom, self-determination: it is power." Henri Frederic Amiel

If you have discipline, it means you take control of your own actions. It allows you to choose to do the right thing; especially when it's difficult. If you don't have discipline you can end up with a great many difficulties. People who are discipline problems have little self-control. Since they cannot control their own behavior, they are disciplined by those in authority. They become powerless instead of powerful.

Instead of thinking of discipline as something bad, think of it as something good and helpful. Think of discipline as a tool to help you reach your goals. Discipline is what allows you to stop your actions.

When you want to do something you know is wrong, discipline serves as the brakes. In the cafeteria when you feel like throwing something, discipline stops you. When it's late at night and you want to eat junk food, discipline helps you to put the chips down. When you don't feel like planning for the day ahead, discipline helps you to prepare. When you are driving while texting instead of paying attention, discipline helps you stay focused. When it's fourth and one and you want to crush the ball carrier, discipline helps you stay onsides. When you are in an argument and want to say something particularly mean, discipline helps you keep those thoughts to yourself. These are all different situations but they all involve you and your level of self-discipline. Practicing self-discipline will help you in all situations. Put the cell phone away, step away from the chips, and say no to the beer or the bud at a party.

"By constant self-discipline and self-control, you can develop greatness. "-Grenville Kleiser

Stop trying to take The Easy Way in everything you do! This destroys your discipline. I often tell my players and students, "Just because you can, doesn't make it right." Just because there isn't a cop around, or your boss doesn't hold you accountable does not make what you are doing right. In fact you are hurting your own discipline. The best part of discipline is that it is something you can always improve upon. Not only that, but once your discipline gets stronger in a given area you find it easier to be disciplined in all aspects of your life.

Your discipline is like a muscle. The more exercise it gets, the stronger it will become. In a culture that provides anything you want, anytime you want it, you simply must have strong discipline or you will suffer suffocation from overabundance of things easily gained. It pays to avoid the shortcut and sometimes very purposefully take the long way, the hard way, the more difficult and less comfortable path. It will help you to grow your discipline. All of those actions will help cultivate your discipline on and off the field. You will feel a great sense of power and achievement even in the smallest instance when you choose The Character Way instead of The Easy Way.

Likewise, when you have to get something done that you don't want to do, discipline is the gas pedal. In the fast food restaurant when you drop your napkin, discipline is what makes you pick it up. When you do not feel like going to school or lifting or work, discipline gets you where you need to be. Discipline keeps you on those train tracks towards your goal. It helps you achieve things when you want to be a lazy bum. Get your homework done, clean up after yourself, and you are more likely to get in the weight room when you should. The best teams in any sport are usually the most disciplined, but so too are the best students.

An important aspect of discipline is focus. Can you identify some things that cause you to lose focus when you are studying? How can you create a working environment that will help you to stay focused? If you lose focus in a meeting and miss something important how will this affect the team's chances for success? What will you do when you feel you are losing focus? What will you do when you see your teammates losing focus?

The first step in staying focused is to determine what you want to stay focused on. What are your goals? What do you want to accomplish? Identifying these things will give you something to care about and stay focused on. This will propel and channel your efforts.

An important aspect of staying focused is to identify potential distractions ahead of time. This gets back to the old saying that those who fail to plan, plan to fail. If you can figure out what might distract you, you might be able to better focus on what you need to do to be successful.

Sometimes we call this forethought.

I'll give you an example where seemingly small losses of focus have cost us victories. The end of the school year in lacrosse is much like Thanksgiving week for football. There are large assemblies in the gym and other related events like Powder Puff, senior field trips, assemblies and dances that most of our players attend and participate in. There is nothing wrong with any of these events, but if you want to win on Thanksgiving or win in the playoffs in lacrosse where should your main focus be? Keep your focus on the games and you have a great chance to win. Get caught up in the other stuff and you are setting yourself up for failure.

Summer is a great time. Nobody loves summer more than me. But if our players lose focus that first day of football practice will be there before they can prepare for it. They have to keep an appropriate amount of focus on lifting and running and on going to camps. That doesn't mean they can't have any fun, but if they don't keep fixed on football during the summer, it will be too late come August. Within the first two weeks of lifting they will have had almost 1,200 repetitions in the weight room. That's a lot to miss, and that is just within two weeks out of a typical nine week summer vacation.

In school, during the final week of regular classes most teachers give their students a final exam review sheet and some class time to study for exams. When I look around our classrooms few of those kids are utilizing this time as productively as they could. Despite the best effort of our teachers too many students focus on their social life. A key to success is to avoid falling into these traps.

Stay focused on what's most important for you to achieve your goals. We all have a tendency to forget to tie what we are doing in the moment to what we want to achieve in the future. As such, we need to remind ourselves. In my personal struggles I have four or five things I have to remind myself of at least twice a day. If I don't do this I will resort to The Easy Way and fall into damaging behaviors. In order to remain on The Character Way I pick a place I drive by during my commute to work and remind myself about my goals and the behaviors I need to avoid. On my way home I remind myself again. Even on the days I do not have to go to work, I take some time each morning and afternoon to remind myself.

In order to remind our players about the importance of building their character I put posters of quotes up all around our weight room. I also copy those posters and ask them to put them up somewhere they will see them on a daily basis like their mirror or locker. The bottom line is that we must constantly remind ourselves of our long term goals in order to keep them fresh in our heads when we are making our daily decisions.

Many of us ritually make our list of things to accomplish each day; but have you made your list of things to not accomplish? Like many, I find myself doing things I don't really need or want to do. I tend to remember things, so I'm pretty protective about what I expose my mind to, but sometimes I find myself watching unappealing TV shows. Other times, actually many times, I eat for no reason. I will also drink another cup of coffee when I don't really want to. A more recent example was when I found myself letting someone take up too much of my time with idle conversations I didn't gain much from.

Much is made of taking a positive approach. But the positive is only one perspective, and is the truth of something not better discovered by viewing it from as many perspectives as possible? Sometimes it might be wise to take the negative approach (To don't). If I eliminate the things I don't want to do today, I will most certainly free some of my day for other pursuits. I will fill that time with something I like, or even better, discover something new to like.

During warm-ups for a huge lacrosse playoff game we had players missing their equipment, fixing their sticks etc. These players were great competitors all year. Their focus had allowed us to gain the number one seed in the district tournament. However, they certainly had lost focus in the hours before the game and were not prepared for what would become a very close loss. Our season abruptly ended that day because of a lack of focus before the game even started.

In order to start properly the intensity of caring has to build prior to the occasion. I have found that the time immediately before an event is pivotal. Our players struggle mightily before lacrosse games. We play twenty of them each season and we tend to lose our focus at some point. We show up before a game giddy and unfocused and find ourselves down by a few goals before we wake up and get going. Those early leads often prove insurmountable. At some point the happy go lucky silliness needs to end and the game faces need to go on. I despised having to continuously address this issue year after year. I wanted to coach the game, not have to be the bad guy and rip into everyone to get serious, like our better opponents always seemed to be, before the game.

One year we incorporated something new into our pre-game routine. We would leave about ten minutes between warm-ups and the start of the game. Our players would gather in a secluded corner of the field. Once there each player would stand in front of the team and commit to something he would do during the game. It could be scoring a specific number of goals, but more importantly it might be forcing a turnover, or hustling to a loose ball before the opponent. The players, who know they might not get in the game much, might commit to making sure the water bottles are filled or playing the spare minutes they might get with great enthusiasm and intensity. This commitment is really about clarifying what we care about and putting it in the front of our mind. When a player tells twenty-five of his teammates he is going to do something just prior to a game, it puts some pressure on him to remember he has to get it done.

A good time to start getting the game face on is when you are putting your business or sports shoes on. Incorporating a little symbolism when you are lacing them up for a day at the office or for the game might prove helpful in remembering what you care about. On each shoe is an inside lace and an outside lace. On the left foot the outside lace is winning. The inside lace is a reason you have inside yourself for wanting to win. This is a selfish reason. Something you care about just for you. Tie the winning lace to that internal reason you want to do well. On the right foot the inside lace is the winning lace. The outside lace is a reason someone outside of you wants to succeed. This could be a reason related to family, team, or community. Tie the outside lace to the winning lace. Once you have tied these inside and outside reasons to winning you will be focused on what you care about and ready to kick some tail.

11
PERSEVERENCE

"The beauty of the soul shines out when a man bears with composure
one heavy mischance after another,
not because he does not feel them,
but because he is a man of high and heroic temper."-Aristotle

When I was thirteen I watched a boxing match. I didn't know that fight would change my life. I grew up about a half hour away from where famed boxer Larry Holmes lived in Easton, PA. I was well versed in his career and had seen many of his bouts on television. I had even eaten at one of his restaurants. When I turned the television on there he was, only a little bit into the first round of the fight. He was facing some shaggy haired guy who looked like he had just gotten off his shift at the mill, gone to the bar for a few cold ones and showed up to challenge the heavyweight champion of the world. What I saw during the rest of the fight would change my life.

Holmes pounded the other guy over and over again. The challenger rarely threw any punches and soon his face was swollen. Howard Cosell was announcing the fight and though I didn't understand most of what he said, it was obvious that Cosell thought the fight should be stopped before the contender was seriously injured. But the fight went on and on; round after round of the pummeling continued. Holmes gave it his all but could not get this other guy to quit or run away. As the fight went on I stopped cheering for Holmes and started rooting for this other guy to make it to the final bell that would ring at the conclusion of the fifteenth round. Long story short, he made it.

Randall "Tex" Cobb taught me a valuable lesson that I have never forgotten and have often celebrated. At the end of the fight he looked at Holmes and smiled. The message was clear. There is great honor to be found in never giving up even if you get your ass kicked in front of everyone. Standing toe to toe against a superior adversary and simply not allowing that adversary to break your will and make you quit or run away is the finest measure of a man. Holmes could out skill, out punch and out move Cobb, but he couldn't out tough him.

When events are pushing you forward do you push back or do you push forward? Anyone can quit something hard. Through character & mental toughness we learn to stick with the hard & quit the easy. Then we get better. We all have had moments when a voice inside our head tells us to take the easy way and give up. Ignoring this voice takes mental toughness. The more mental toughness you have, the more successful you will be. The desire to quit will come. It can be very powerful in its justifications. Most people fall for it. You have to be prepared for it. Where do you quit? Before you even start? When it gets tough? Do you quit at the finish line, final whistle, or last buzzer? If you force yourself to do one thing, make it to the end, then you will often find you gave more than you ever thought you could.

We have players on our team that I call S and S players. They only practice when it's sunny and seventy. Rain, cold, heat, snow, an aggressive breeze and these guys are drawn to the trainer's golf cart. They made up their minds before practice they were going to quit early for the day, they just had to find a time when few people would notice.

In previous chapters we have talked about the many distractions and adversities our players have to overcome, but there are few worse than the officials. Young people have a profound sense of justice and when an official blows a call, or decides that he will throw his flag for the first time on the turning point play of the game, our players are mentally lost. I tell our guys outright that we will have to beat our opponent and the officials too. That's just the way it is. Poor officiating is unfortunately more common than we would like. However, complaining about the refs is like complaining about the weather. You can cry and scream and complain all you want, it won't change the weather. The same goes for the referee. Worse, allowing the officiating to distract you keeps you from focusing on what you can control. Complaining about officials is a true sign of mental weakness. Besides, most of the officials are very dedicated and their calls are correct; even the ones against you. But in football we have at least five officials working each game and one of them is bound to be pretty weak or have poor character

When I was fighting those court battles, I found injustice was common. I could write a compelling book about the inequities and indifference I faced in working through the legal system. In the hallways at court I heard people complain constantly. In watching proceedings before my own would take place, some complainers had no reason to protest, but others had plenty of evidence on which to base their gripes. But complaining was not going to get me out of a terrible marriage nor allow me to spend more time with my children. Instead I focused on what I could do to help me reach my goals.

We love to use car and tractor tires as part of our summer training program. At least a few times a summer those tires get pretty juicy. After a heavy down pour those tires contain an elixir of mythical proportions; tire water. This potion can only be applied by running tires, throwing tires, flipping tires etc. Once applied to the skin and clothing it has the effect of making a person more mentally tough. It's awesome to see a young man overcome his fear of tire water, not allow it to break his will and come to celebrate its existence.

"Keep on beginning and failing. Each time you fail, start all over again, and you will grow stronger until you have accomplished a purpose – not the one you began with perhaps, but one you'll be glad to remember."
-Anne Sullivan

"People seldom see the halting and painful steps by which the most insignificant success is achieved."
-Anne Sullivan

If it takes little to defeat you, you will have little. If it takes much to defeat you, you will have much. To be a teacher is to be cranky at times. The frustrations of educators are well covered elsewhere, so I will save you from another airing. Teacher Anne Sullivan can be cranky in her writing. I much prefer the words of Anne's famed student to those of Anne, but Anne means more to me for a less obvious reason.

Have you ever passed by a place where you previously spent time alone; confused and lost? I have a place like that. It was near an apartment complex I lived in. It's a sparse little park that takes up one corner of a busy intersection. At night I would go for walks until my legs just about gave out and then I would stop in that park before I would go back to my apartment and try to sleep. In my travels I drive by that park sometimes. More often than not I hit a red light at that intersection. I look over and I see myself sitting there years before; alone at night, on the nondescript bench, as lost as lost could be. Sometimes my heart aches to console the guy I once was; sitting there alone, tortured by inescapable thoughts night after night; trying desperately to find my way out of the intricate and treacherous maze my life had become. I want to tell that former version of me that it will work out. Not perfect, but alright, far more good than bad. I don't want to tell myself the whole story, but just enough to take away the depths of gut wrenching confusion and hopelessness.

Other times I'm stopped at that intersection and I can't help but smile. For 90 seconds I remember how far I've come. I drive away grateful as the light turns green. In that little park is a statue of Anne Sullivan, Helen Keller's teacher. I never talked to Anne on those lonesome nights. But some nights she spoke to me. She said "keep trying, don't give up, it's possible; you're going to break through." She gave me hope that tomorrow might be better. Some nights her words brought true solace and I could walk back to that apartment and sleep a bit.

"My heart is singing for joy this morning! A miracle has happened!
The light of understanding has shone upon my little pupil's mind,
and behold, all things are changed!"
Anne Sullivan

I know Anne was speaking of her other student when she wrote this in her journal, but she might have meant me. She found a way to help me see and hear what I couldn't at that difficult time in my life. Through her I was reminded that miracles do happen if you never give up.

The will is your best tool in fighting to persevere. We all have one. But we need to find a way to tap into it, to summon and strengthen it. In order to get my players to recognize this I wrote them the following piece.

IMPOSE YOUR WILL

Your will is stronger than you can imagine. Your will is incredibly powerful. Impose your will. Don't wait to have the will. You already have it. Impose your will. Don't look around for it, that's a waste of time. It's already there. Impose your will. Can't seem to start working out? Impose your will. Can't seem to pay attention to your work or studies? Impose your will. Can't say no to dessert? Impose your will. Stuck in a bad situation? Impose your will. Say it! **IMPOSE YOUR WILL!**

When you impose your will you summon all of your resources and use them to your advantage. You find an intensity and focus that can force you to achieve your goals. When you impose your will you discover inner depths of strength you were never aware of. When you impose your will you can achieve things you thought were impossible.

When you impose your will you sublimate all the feelings that get in the way of your achieving what you want to achieve. When you impose your will, you blast right past those feelings and tap into the power of your soul.

I once wrote that the thing I was most petrified of was my own will.

It's terrifying to know you are capable of anything. Usually that type of statement carries negative connotations and that might be part of the fear. I know I could impose my will to lift something I have no business lifting. I know I could impose my will in an effort to jump from a great height, or swim a great distance. Obviously these things could lead me to great trouble. So I have to be cognizant about when I impose my will. To know you have the will to attempt anything is scary. Thankfully, I have been pretty smart about imposing my will through the years.

But I also know I can impose my will in the positive sense. I have imposed my will to accomplish things I could never imagine accomplishing; working a ridiculous amount of hours, performing at a ridiculous level, attacking problems that must be addressed or sustaining a high tempo over a long period of time.

Coaches sometimes talk about their team imposing their will on another team. But I don't think that's true. What is true is that you can impose your will on yourself; on your own thoughts and feelings. By imposing your will on yourself, you summon the strength, stamina, character and mental toughness necessary to defeat your opponent. The opponent loses and you are victorious because you have imposed your will and competed to the very best of your abilities.

No team has imposed their will on another; no more than a person might impose their will on another. Instead they have imposed their will on themselves and found the power to achieve what they want to achieve. Teams imposing their will discover an intensity and focus that rivals can't match because those rivals have not imposed their own will.

Don't find your will. That's like finding a tool but never using it. Impose your will. You already have the tool; put it to work for you! Impose your will. I know I can, so I know you can. Tomorrow when the alarm goes off at 5 AM, rather than hitting the snooze the first thing I will tell myself is **IMPOSE YOUR WILL!** Tomorrow when you want to do something and are having trouble getting started or finishing say to yourself **IMPOSE YOUR WILL!**

"The enemy determines when you rest."- Joseph Joffre

Joffre was the commander of the French military at the beginning of WWI. Vastly outnumbered by the German attackers, Joffre ordered a retreat of French forces over hundreds of miles. His goal was to regroup and then once again go on the offensive. When the time came to once again go on the attack, one of the generals beneath Joffre protested saying his troops needed more time to rest before regaining the offensive. This is the point where Joffre uttered those famous words.

So who, or what, is your enemy and how does it determine when you rest? Your enemy may be a project that is due, an opponent you will face in the fall, a workout session you have to get through. You may want to rest, but before you do, maybe you should consider your enemy first. The project may need to get done now. This will require that you do not rest until your work is done. The opponent you will face in the fall is working out today. This will require that you do not rest until after your workout is done.

It is in these moments when projects become a success or failure. It is in these moments when games are won or lost well before they are even played. Don't ever fool yourself into thinking that what you do, or don't do today will have no bearing on whether you succeed or fail at some later point. Today is important. Today is a chance to get better. Either you or the enemy will realize that and act accordingly. Your laziness today is your loss tomorrow. Your work today is your win tomorrow. How much further from who you were yesterday can you get today? You may want to take a break, but if your enemy isn't going to take a break, you have to find the mental toughness to keep going. So the next time you feel like taking The Easy Way remind yourself of ole' Joffre's words.

The reward for perseverance is often victory. But if you can finish the contest having given it your all, and not allowing someone or something to break you, then you will be rewarded with pride. Pride and confidence come from achieving something difficult. Let that sink in for a moment. Pride does not come from doing something easy. Real confidence does not come from doing something easy. Pride and confidence come from doing something hard. Only then can we look back and look at what we achieved. Only then can we have confidence from knowing we are capable of fighting through difficulty. Pride and confidence are developed slowly. They come from completing tough work each day.

Nobody walks into the weight room their first time with pride and confidence. We gain pride and confidence from showing up and letting our teammates and ourselves know that we can be counted on. Pride and confidence come from knowing that we have gotten a little stronger each day and that we have not allowed the workout to break our will.

Nobody shows up on their first day of football with pride and confidence. Each practice is a battle; a battle to just show up; a battle to learn techniques; a battle to take a hit and keep going; a battle to play smart under pressure. When you walk off the field after a hard practice, knowing you have gotten better from surviving those battles, that's when pride comes.

There is a significant amount of people that believe you gain confidence from completing easy tasks. They advocate little baby steps of ease; with a trophy for each little step. They believe these build your confidence or, as they like to call, it self-esteem. But that's a lie. Sooner or later you will have to face a true challenge. If you have not previously challenged yourself, then you will be overcome and your will is likely to be broken. True confidence will only come from straining to complete something difficult. Only then will you know that you deserve to feel confident. You see confidence is nothing more than extinguishing your fears. If all you ever take are little baby steps of ease, you will remain afraid. Overcome your uncertainty through hard work and toughness and the confidence and pride will flow through you. Get to the point where you can say "I may be defeated, but nothing and no one can break me," and actually believe it.

12
INITIATIVE

"To them life appears as a fixed condition, which man has no power to alter. Endowed with little initiative, too much inclined to look upon themselves as minors and in tutelage, they are quick to believe in destiny and resign themselves to it."- Ernest Renan

"You must not only aim aright, but draw the bow with all your might."
-Henry David Thoreau

Later is a big part of lateral, advance now or your options may not include moving forward. I have been coaching for quite some time. I have coached over twenty football seasons. I have coached fifteen lacrosse seasons. I coached a half dozen basketball seasons as well. I have coached Division 1 college ball all the way to high school freshmen and the grade school kids I have in camps. One thing always amazes me. No matter the sport, no matter the level, no matter the gender, I am always amazed at how many players simply settle. They settle for just being on the team instead of being in the game. They settle for just being in the game instead of being a factor in the game. They settle for letting a teammate work harder than them in practice and earn more playing time at their expense. They settle for letting an opposing player at another school work harder than them and earn the spot on the post-season all-star team. The same can be said of teams. Too many teams feel they cannot compete for championships or that other teams are somehow more deserving.

There are a variety of reasons this happens. But one of those reasons I will no longer abide by on the teams I coach. No longer will players be unaware they are settling. From now on they will know better. From now on I will ask them two questions. Why not you? Why not now? These will not be rhetorical questions. While I may give them some time to answer, I will want to hear their answer. I want them to have to think about why they don't feel they should be a starter or a star. I want them to think about why they want to wait for success to come to them rather than enjoying it right now. Hopefully, this will help them to recognize that they can achieve more, and that their effort and attitude determines what they get or don't get. Hopefully, they will earn their dream every day, starting today.

"Our real duty is always found running in the direction of our worthiest desires." —Randolph Bourne

Nobody is going to hand you playing time at the varsity level in high school. Nobody is going to hand you an all star nomination. The same holds true in school and in life. Nobody is going to hand you an "A." Nobody is going to walk up and give you a great job or promotion. Nobody will hand you an honorable discharge or a college degree. You have to go on the attack right now, and go get what you want; you; now. That's the first step of a great player. That's the first step of a great team. That's the first step of a great student or soldier or employee. That's the first step in changing from someone who wants it to happen to someone who is making it happen. Why not you? Why not now? Why settle when you could be earning your dream?

There are certain things in football (and in life) that are mandatory. For example: you must have a physical before you practice, you must wear the proper equipment, you must go to practice in order to play in varsity games, you must pay your sports fee, you must obey the rules. Those are all mandatory. You have to do them.

The rest of football is optional, meaning things you don't have to do. Examples are lifting weights, running, going to camps, working on your character and mental toughness, giving a great effort, working on your technique and skills, helping your teammates get better. Nobody can force you to do those things. They are optional.

The mandatory stuff decides whether or not you play football. The optional stuff decides whether you, and the team, will be any good at football. Players that do the optional things, and do them well, are far better off than players who only do the mandatory things.

Character & mental toughness are so important because once you have them, you will do the optional. If you don't have character you will only do the mandatory. If you do not have mental toughness you will only do the optional when it is easy, or convenient, or you feel like it.

One day of blowing off the optional leads to days of blowing off the optional. This leads to weeks and years of blowing off the optional. This leaves you way behind those with character and mental toughness at your school or business and other schools and businesses. This will leave you, and as a result your team, in a pretty bad position come game time. It will be what you do with these options that determine how successful you are in life.

If you only do what is mandatory, you are not likely going to get very far. Success in life is optional. Do more, get more. Do less, get less. Do what you have always done, you will never have more than what you always had. Mandatory defines your team, your school or workplace, your organization. Optional defines the success of those things. Mandatory is easy. Optional is hard.

Can you help me figure something out? I'm a teacher with four kids. I mow my own lawn. When I'm done, I kick back and enjoy the results. If it were in my budget to have someone mow it for me, I would probably pay someone to do it. I would still enjoy the results. But what if someone mowed it for me and I didn't have to pay them? Not a favor, not a nickel. Would I still enjoy the results? Yes.

Think ahead to the big game, or big promotion, or big addition to your new house. What if there was no way you could lose? What if you had 100% certainty that it would happen? Would you still work hard? I'm sure some of us would say yes. I think most of us would say, however hesitantly, no.

Why would we work hard when we were going to win anyway? Oh sure some of us have it ingrained in our minds that we will work hard. But much of that is because we have been conditioned to take satisfaction from seeing a job well done; we know it is a prerequisite to success. If our effort was no longer tied to success, our effort would soon disappear.

If we know we will win, human nature kicks in and we stop working at the same level. We stop putting up with stress, pain, and inconvenience. Those things have no value if we are going to win anyway.

This idea leads me to four thoughts. The first is when people set the bar so low and strive for so little that they just settle, sometimes for next to nothing. They expect so little of themselves because their win is so easy that it requires no effort. As an example I think about a kid who is just happy to be on the team and doesn't push himself to get playing time or a player with great ability who does nothing in regard to reaching his potential. Likewise, the kid who settles for just barely passing his classes so that he graduates. I see these things every day.

Second, if we give people rewards without effort, they begin to lose respect for effort and the inclination to put forth an effort. I think about my youngest son being given a trophy in his second year of soccer even though his team lost every game and rarely scored a goal. I think about kids getting passed up through schools even though they can barely read or do basic math. I think about demands for equal playing time having little to do with ability.

Third, when we start feeling that it is inevitable that we are going to win, we let up; we stop giving it our all. I can think of many a team at every level being ahead late in the game and letting up, only to lose. I think of the poor people down the street every day at the newspaper store playing the lottery and convinced they will win, instead of doing something for themselves or others. I think about seniors in their last semester giving up on their academics and teams.

Fourth, when we forget about losing it is the same as thinking that we will inevitably win. If we are not concerned with losing we put forth little effort. For an example I think of players who do not train in the off-season or kids who do not study for tests. See, losing drives me nuts. It drives me way more so than winning. I hate to lose; at anything ever. Is that because I have some innate sense of pride? Or is it that I focus on losing?

I look at some of the people I coach and teach. I look at some of the people in the community. I wonder why these people have so little pride. But then maybe I think it's not pride; it's just one of those four things or a combination of them. They don't set their sights very high so they will win, settling for little. They get rewards for doing little, so they do little. They feel like they are going to win, so they let up. They don't think about losing, so they lose.

I want to reach those people. At least the ones I can. When I don't reach them, particularly my players and students, I feel like I lost. I feel like I let those kids down, my teams down, my school down, and let society down because these people are not contributing to their potential. I hate losing. So what are the answers? What can I do as a teacher or coach to change this?

In a larger sense, what can I do on a larger scale to change that at the community and societal level? I drive around town or pick up a paper and I constantly see people settling, not finishing, being rewarded for doing little, and not giving thought to their inevitable losses. Don't tell me little or nothing. I won't believe you. I cannot accept that. I hate losing.

So here are a few of my answers. First, challenge people to be the best they can be. Help them to recognize their potential. Give them examples of how other people have realized their potential and done great things. Challenge students in class and players in practice. Let them know when they could be doing better. Recognize the times they actually do work to their potential so they can see what they are capable of.

Second, don't give rewards for things that are not earned. I actually did this in the fall. I refused to let my son have his trophy. Bless her heart, my wife even supported me. A couple of months later my son found it and promptly gave it to his little sister. I am a fortunate man.

Third, push people to maintain a consistent high quality effort and require them to finish what they start. Encourage people to not quit a team or stop doing homework until it's complete. Make teams finish their drills and practices. Train players not to relax until the success is actually achieved. Give them examples of situations where people have quit trying right before they were about to succeed.

Fourth, consistently remind people about what is at stake. Remind them of how much losing (failing a class, losing a starting spot, losing a game, being passed over for a promotion etc.) is miserable. Put it right in front of them. Allow them to lose and make sure they know when they do so they can learn the hard lesson.

I accept that I am limited in my influence on young people. If a parent is not on the same page as me and holding up their end in these pursuits then I stand little chance of success. The only other way a kid can succeed is for him to hold up the other side of the vice on his own. Likewise, on a larger level I can only make people aware and try to hold up my side of the vice through my words and my actions.

I'm glad we have opportunities to reap the benefits of hard work. I am grateful for the many fine people I know who work extremely hard. But I remain puzzled about how I can reach people who are so easily satisfied, provided for, give up quickly, and could care less, at least for now, whether they win or lose. I know I reach many by doing the things that I do, but I feel there must be a means of reaching more.

"You may never know what results come of your actions,
but if you do nothing, there will be no results." – Gandhi

Maybe it's because I have survived cancer and feel the clock ticking with uncertainty. Maybe it's because I am impatient. Maybe it's because I am wicked competitive. Maybe it's a habit from all these years of coaching. I don't really know. What I do know is that I am obsessed with getting myself and others better. Sometimes I do this in profound ways and on other occasions only a fraction at a time. I have an overwhelming sense of urgency about this. It has become, more than anything, what I do. It has become me.

As such, I feel like my time is precious. I feel like every spare minute presents an opportunity to get myself and others better. It's as if I were in a race with an undetermined finish line. At some unknown moment the horn will blow and that will be it. The victory decided by how far I have traveled and helped others travel in the time that's been allotted. How far we go is determined by how efficiently we use our time and how much meaning we inject into each moment.

I know this annoys the hell out of people. Maybe most people are right and I should be more frivolous. Maybe they are wrong and just resent me because they see me and realize the time they waste. I don't know who is right. But in the end I will have made as much of a difference as I could. When the final buzzer sounds I will have traveled some distance and though I will no longer be able to get better my echoes, however loud or feint, will endure.

I have invented little. I have invested much. I have taken the initiative to help people reach their potential. My trophies are people. My dividends are lives lived a little more deeply. Is that so bad?

Over the years my players always seem to struggle with some little things. I will give you one example; the water bottles. We may have a team of 30 or 40 kids. Before they go out to practice, they all know we need water bottles. The caddy with the water bottles weighs about 2 pounds. But they will not bring the water bottles out to practice unless they are directly told to by a coach. Let that sink in for minute; 30 to 40 kids. All of them will walk right by this caddy as they exit the locker room. Not one of them can pick it up. Not one. Day after day.

When the time comes at practice for the players to get a drink of water they all look around and gripe that nobody took the water bottles out to practice. This scene repeats day after day after day. I'm not going to ask you why that is. I already know the answer. What I will ask is why we settle for being so much less than we can be? What I will ask is why this type of behavior is so common? What I will ask is what you are doing to change it in yourself and others?

Memorial Day arrives near the end of our regular lacrosse season. If there is any day of the year that can teach us to recognize that pursuing our own selfish interests is nothing admirable, this should be the day. This should be the day when we realize that we are at our best when we put other people before us. We are at our best when we serve, not expect to be served. This should be the day when we learn to bravely overcome our fear of doing simple little tasks as we realize the tremendous sacrifices others have made. This is the day we should look at those who gave their lives and then look in the mirror and recognize that we ourselves give so very little in comparison. This is the day when we can refuse to be small people of small effort.

I am not encouraging anyone to sign up for military service. That is a personal choice. What I am encouraging is that you sign up for service. No contract to sign. No appointment to make. No group to join. Rather each day make a little effort. Do something that benefits someone other than you. Not because you have to, but because you realize the world is not just about you, and each day you want to confirm that to the world.

While each of those kids will not bring those water bottles out, there always seems to be a couple that will bring them in. Not because they are told to, but because they will not ignore work that needs to be done. They will not pretend that they didn't see the water bottles. They will not pretend they forgot. Those kids know they are better for taking some initiative. Those kids realize a little extra work won't hurt them. Those kids realize they are better for stepping up. Even in a small way. Those guys give me hope and inspire me. I never want to be too good to carry a water bottle.

> *The smallest effort is not lost,*
> *Each wavelet on the ocean tost*
> *Aids in the ebb-tide or the flow;*
> *Each rain-drop makes some floweret blow;*
> *Each struggle lessens human woe.*
> -Charles Mackay

We were at an eating club at Princeton University; a place where I was given a small room as compensation for my internship with the football program. It was Christmas break and all of the students had scattered across the country to their homes. That basically left me alone in a mansion for a couple of weeks. My thoughts never ventured far from the fact that I was temporarily living in some small aspect of a fairy tale. Tens of thousands of square feet, all the amenities and I had it all to myself.

Soon, Kevin, my best friend from high school, joined me for a weekend in my new mansion. We spent some time walking the barren Ancient Eight campus, crawling through the old pubs in town and watching games from easy chairs in the enormous great room. We had the conversations best friends recently out of college have. We spoke of old times and our dreams for the future.

I was on track to becoming a big time college football coach. He was on his way to fulfilling his high school promise of having a big house with an in-ground pool filled with beer and ice. Only that weekend found us a bit disillusioned and moderately derailed. I loved coaching at such a great university but I felt as though my contributions were minimal. The players I coached already had their act together. I couldn't do much to better their lives.

I also found the off the field work tedious. In one coaches' meeting, we spent a couple of hours debating whether a receiver should run a pass route by climbing from 5 to 7 yards or by climbing from 8 to 10. Coaching football was supposed to be about fun, competition and changing people's lives. That meeting left me feeling like I had signed up for the soul sucking cubicle prison I had vowed to never enter; the kind of work that made my father and my friends' fathers come home so miserable from their evening commutes back from New York City. I knew this would be my one and only year of (semi) big time football. I knew I wanted to escape and teach, but I still had no education credentials, only a bachelor's degree in History.

My friend had a perfect math score on his SAT. He could engage in mortal verbal combat with the best our upbringing in New Jersey brought to bear. But he too was lost. He didn't get into his first choice of business schools. He was stuck in a worthy, yet, undistinguished entry level corporate job. He too yearned to make his mark.

We were both contemplating our next steps. At one point that weekend, I don't remember when, I said something to him that he said had a huge impact on his life. Many a time since then he has told me it was the best piece of advice he has received.

My friend and I traded texts the other day. He has done well for himself. He has a very nice family. He also has the type of job he always wanted. He is a partner in a financial firm; the kind of firm that brings him to the upper floors of mid-town Manhattan.

Many times he has told me that he has repeated the advice I gave him long ago. Most recently in a presentation on career advice to roughly 100 people at a corporate function. He swears it has made a huge impact on other people's lives as he has relayed it through the years. He said he told all those people that even if you take just a half a step forward to where you want to go you are making progress towards your goal.

See sometimes we want to make huge strides and we get hugely disappointed when we can't. We feel our dreams slipping away. In those moments we lose ourselves, we get frustrated and scared and we settle or give up. But even if you take the initiative to just get a little better, a little further down the road, the dream lives on.

I still think what I said that weekend, or at least my getting any credit for it, is overrated. But when you hear from a guy who has reached the top of his profession, a guy who shares that piece of advice he got from one of his buddies to a hundred high achievers; well, I begin to think there just might be something to it.

Just focus on narrowing the gap between who you are and who you want to be. Keep moving forward; even a small step in the general direction of your goal is progress towards where you want to go and keeps the dream alive.

13
COMMITMENT

"He who learns must suffer"- Aeschylus

A commitment is a pledge or agreement to do something. That commitment can be with other people or even yourself. Commitment is a train on a track chugging along toward a worthy destination.

I am a lousy golfer. The reason for this is quite simple. I have little natural ability and I am unwilling to practice at the golf range or play enough rounds to get good. I lack commitment. There once was a time when I was an ok golfer. But it took a ton of time and effort on my part.

One of my friends has about the same amount of natural ability that I have in golf. But he's a good player. He bought a membership at a local course and plays a few rounds a week in the spring, summer, and fall. He plays when it's rainy. He plays when it's cold. He plays when it's hot and humid. He plays when nobody else will go out. He talks with good golfers and asks them how they got good. He reads golf books and religiously watches golf tournaments on TV. Well, my friend has become quite a golfer. He is now much better than I. The reason is simple. He is committed.

Did my friend go fishing to become a better golfer? No. He committed to becoming a better golfer so he rarely went fishing. He had to sacrifice some of his other leisure activities.

Did my friend buy really expensive clubs to become a better golfer? No. He knew that new clubs would make him look like a good golfer, but only by putting his time in to practicing was he going to play like a good golfer.

Did my friend quit his teaching job to become a better golfer? No. He needed to support his family. He even got a promotion. He just managed his time well. He kept things in perspective and never let his commitment become ridiculous or damaging.

Did my friend take steroids to become a better golfer? No. Even though he is not very big or strong, he knew that true satisfaction only comes from working hard toward a worthy goal.

Did my friend say he was going to be the next Tiger Woods? No. Anybody can talk about winning. Not everyone can make a commitment. My friend focused on becoming the best player he could be. That was his goal.

"The chains of habit are too weak to be felt until they are too strong to be broken." –
Samuel Johnson

Commitment is the difference between a wish and a goal. Do you wish to be an elite athlete or do you work hard to make sure it happens? Do you wish to have a nice home for your family or do you make sure it happens? The difference is in the commitment.

Commitment doesn't take breaks or holidays. It doesn't sleep in class. It doesn't leave its notebook in its locker or forget it's pads before practice. It doesn't watch TV and eat Pringles three at time during lifting hours. It doesn't make excuses.

What you commit to now will show up later. Committed to eating junk food and watching TV? I bet you know how that turns out. Committed to just getting by in school? I bet you know how that turns out.

Don't expect to become a great golfer if you spend all your time fishing.

"I wish to preach, not the doctrine of ignoble ease, but the doctrine of the strenuous life, the life of toil and effort, of labor and strife; to preach that highest form of success which comes, not to the man who desires mere easy peace, but to the man who does not shrink from danger, from hardship, or from bitter toil, and who out of these wins the splendid ultimate triumph. A life of slothful ease, a life of that peace which springs merely from lack either of desire or of power to strive after great things, is as little worthy of a nation as of an individual."- Theodore Roosevelt

In my many years of coaching I found that most of the problems I dealt with were related to commitment. Too many of my players and students were not committed to athletic or academic achievement. To make matters worse, both those young people and their parents expected success to come with expedient ease. So in order to explain to them the prolonged cost of achievement I wrote the following piece and shared it with them.

The Process & Levels of Commitment

Commitment Process Step 1 –Play or Quit

Very simply a person must decide whether or not they want to play. Playing has its costs and rewards. The player must sacrifice some of their free time activities and their comfort. There is great fear in making this initial decision. They may not know specifics but they know they will be called upon to work hard and endure pain. Even more terrifying is the idea of having to be counted on. Most people will not play football. Many others will try but do not last very long.

"{Donkeys} would rather have straw than gold."-Heraclitus

"Very often a change of self is needed more than a change of scene."
-Arthur Christopher Benson

"It is your attitude at the beginning of a difficult undertaking which, more than anything else, will determine its successful outcome."-William James

Commitment Process Step 2 –Semi Commit

After the player decides to play, they semi-commit. They find that being on the team is rewarding, but they are trying to figure out how to get the reward with a minimal amount of sacrifice. This player practices reasonably hard when it is 60-75 degrees but hesitates when it becomes hotter or colder or wetter out. This person lifts weights when it is convenient for them, or when they can find nothing better to do. This person avoids the more strenuous lifts, or only does some of the lifts the coach asks the team to do. This player looks for opportunities to miss the occasional practice, misses reps in practice, runs sprints but not to their fullest potential. This player will sit out with the slightest hurt. This player usually is in the back of the line during drills. They try to match themselves up against similar or even weaker competition during practices. This player will occasionally look like they have achieved the next step, but eventually it is revealed to be a fleeting flash of potential. They really spend most of their time trying to get by and little time trying to get better. Eventually they will get called upon to do the growing up required to take the next step.

"Everyone confesses that exertion which brings out all the powers of body and mind is the best thing for us; but most people do all they can to get rid of it,

and as a general rule nobody does much more than circumstances drive them to do. Human nature is above all things lazy."-Harriet Beecher Stowe

"Nobody likes the man who brings bad news"-Sophocles in Antigone

Note of Caution:

The next step is the step that parents often have the most difficulty with their son or daughter taking. The reason for this is because their child's character flaws must first be highlighted in such a way that he can no longer deny them. He will inevitably be placed in a position where he must make a decision to either fix his flaws or live with the consequences. For example, if he does not hustle he will not play, if he forgets his equipment he will not play, if he goes offsides or forgets his plays he will be letting the team down and we will lose. The player will have no one to blame but his own lack of character and mental toughness. These shortcomings will be noticed.

While we try our best to offer positive lessons, sometimes the negative aspect of events and their corresponding consequences must also be taught. These are no less a part of truth than the positive, and can be a vital part of development.

Like an animal still sporting its winter coat as summer approaches, the time for change has come and it is often confusing and difficult for everyone involved. The player has gone as far as he can with his current mindset and must begin to grow in areas he may formerly have been unaware of. The Easy Way no longer takes him where he wishes to go. Rather than maturing and taking The Character Way, he complains about his failure resulting from things being too hard, or unfair.

The parental instinct to shield the child from difficulty often prevents the child from taking the next step which is often very hard to take. The child may become quiet or sullen as he contemplates his next step or he may come home seeking sympathy by claiming that the coach was "mean to him".

The child often over dramatizes the words or context of what a coach or teammate said and fails to report the many supportive comments that the coaches or teammates have made. Ironically, educators often are on the reciprocal side of this, where a parent has recognized an area that needs growth and the child seeks out sympathy from the coach or teacher.

The parent likely feels the need to console the son who comes home feeling sorry for himself after having his flaw revealed. Sometimes the parent reacts by lashing out at the person who has recognized the child's character flaw and called for improvement.

This is understandable; no parent wants their child to be unhappy. But the goal is for the player to become a fine young man. If the parent does not permit the child to change, to improve, then the child will remain a child. Growing is by definition changing, and recognizing and making that change is difficult. The character flaw of a poor work ethic, lack of courage, irresponsibility, lack of accountability, lack of respect for other people or property etc. will never change if the player is not permitted to learn any lesson that is uncomfortable or difficult.

Worse, the child will be denied the opportunity to grow truly confident, the type of confidence that comes only from having the courage to face their flaws and fears and then overcome them.

So please be aware that growing up is difficult and that becoming something special, a man of character and mental toughness who can be counted on in any situation, is even more difficult. However, in the end, that young man will take pride in himself and you will be proud of what a fine person he has become.

"Fall seven times, get up eight." – Japanese Proverb

*"The gem cannot be polished without friction,
nor man perfected without trials." – Chinese Proverb*

"Never give in. Never. Never. Never. Never." – Winston Churchill

*"All truth goes through three phases. First it is ridiculed. Second it is vehemently
opposed. Third it accepted as being self-evident" –Arthur Schopenhauer*

*"If you will call your troubles experiences, and remember that every experience develops
some latent force within you, you will grow vigorous and happy, however adverse your
circumstances may seem to be." John Heywood*

Commitment Process Step 3- Commit to Self

Something happens; usually something unpleasant. The player is now honest with himself. The player suddenly realizes that he is capable of giving much more than he has. He recognizes that being a Semi Commit will not bring him what he desires. This is because being a Semi Commit is taking The Easy Way, which ultimately ends in failure.

The player comes to understand that the harder he works, the better he will be and the more fun he will have. The joy of competition increases exponentially with the investment of one's' self. He begins to seek out responsibility instead of running from it. The player truly accepts that he has flaws in some character areas and makes an extremely powerful decision to seek out and correct these flaws in order to reach his potential.

The player gets a piercing-fierce look in his eye and begins doing not just the work, but the hard work, the type of work that average people can't fathom. The player realizes that this type of effort is not as bad as he feared. The player not only puts in the time, but begins putting great effort into the time he puts in.

He is doing more than he ever imagined. He is now serious and his confidence begins to soar from the empowerment he feels from courageously facing his faults and fears and recognizing that he has the determination within him to persevere and grow into what he dreamed he could be.

The player's family is astounded by the growth and maturity this budding young man exhibits, and usually can't seem to identify the catalyst though they readily testify to the result.

"Eureka!"-Greek for "I have found it!"

Commitment Process Step 4 –Commit to others

This player keeps himself on The Character Way. He has displayed consistent character and mental toughness. He now begins to utilize his awareness and take initiative. He has an awareness of what the teams needs to do in order to be successful and he accepts responsibility for seeing that it gets done. He is willing to give everything he has towards the cause and is motivated by the fact that others will see this and be inspired to make a similar sacrifice for the good of the team. He begins to take pride in the achievements of others he has guided along The Character Way.

"He who lives by great virtue may be compared to the north star, which keeps its place as all other stars turn towards it."-Confucius

"We awaken in others the same attitude of mind we hold toward them."-Elbert Hubbard

Commitment Process Step 5 –Commit in any situation

The ultimate goal is that the player applies the lessons taught in football to academics, other sports, social situations, employment, family etc. The player recognizes that he can only be one person if he wishes to be successful. He understands that he cannot take The Easy Way in one situation and then The Character Way in the next situation. He begins to adopt The Character Way as a way of life.

His decisions are quicker because he has a sound core from which to refer to and the actions he takes are more profound. He gains momentum, constantly growing and learning. While nobody can ever achieve perfection, he is coming closer and closer to fulfilling his potential in all facets of his life.

He begins to see that love means being there. Love is being there for his family no matter the situation (rich, poor, healthy, sick, etc). Love is being there for their teammates no matter the situation (hot, cold, winning, losing, playing, cheering from the bench etc.). He is becoming someone special; a man of character and mental toughness who can be counted on in any situation.

"When you realize there is nothing lacking, the whole world belongs to you"-Lao Tzu

14
LEADERSHIP

Tzu-chang asked Confucius: "How should men be governed?"
The Master said: "He who would govern men must honour the five graces, spurn the four vices."
Tzu-chang said: "What are the five graces?"
The Master said: "A gentleman is kind, but not wasteful; he burdens, but does not embitter; he is covetous, not sordid; high-minded, not proud; he inspires awe, and not fear."
Tzu-chang said: "What are the four vices?"
The Master said: "To leave untaught and then kill is cruelty: to ask full tale without warning is tyranny: to give careless orders, and be strict when the day comes is robbery: to be stingy in rewarding men is littleness."

Leadership The Character Way is not about exploiting players for wins or personnel for profits. It's about win-win and profit-profit. In helping those you oversee seize opportunities to become more than they thought they could be you will gain from their increased humility, caring, teamwork, effort, courage, discipline, perseverance, initiative and commitment. Their growth in these traits will increase the quality, quantity and duration of their contribution to your cause. Collaborate in developing their character and the celebrations of your group achievement will coincide with their personal triumphs. Many will tell you that a leader needs to have character, and I hope I have helped to illustrate what that means.

"Quality is not an act, it is a habit." –Aristotle

"Dig the well before you are thirsty." – Chinese Proverb

Successful leadership also entails developing peoples' character and mental toughness to their fullest. Strong leaders bring out the best in the people they lead by teaching, modeling, and evoking the character traits. As such I will approach leadership by discussing factors of character and mental toughness as they relate to your need to get people to diligently work together to achieve your mission.

As a leader, your lack of addressing character and mental toughness will catch up with you because character flaws will catch up with the people you lead. The situation will present itself where you or your organization will lose. At the heart of that loss will be a flaw in character and or mental toughness. Might that flaw have been addressed earlier, before the crucial moment when it affected performance? There are a lot of ways to win, but there really is only one way to win consistently. How many more times must we be so busy that we are blinded by these truths? We are willing to hustle; we want desperately to succeed, so why do we continue to ignore the fundamental components of success?

I once heard it said that cement in the Hoover dam is still curing 80 years after construction started. As it cures the cement grows stronger. Your foundation in leading The Character Way is every bit the cement commonly used in building great structures. It will cure with time and grow stronger. You can do much to enliven, invigorate, and expedite that process in yourself and others.

"A tiger doesn't change it's stripes."- Proverb

Don't give up on change. Sure there are tigers, but there are far more caterpillars waiting for you to help them become butterflies. Change is everywhere around us, don't take an excuse that people won't change. People change all the time. Some call it growth. There are plenty of people eager to grow, to rise from their dormancy. Ignite that change in yourself and those you lead. The best part is they will sooner or later be grateful for what you shared with them.

I know full well the story of the scorpion and the frog, but might both the frog and the scorpion have both benefited from growing an awareness of character and mental toughness long before they set off to cross the stream? People can change. People do change. People can help other people see the benefits of change. To say that people can't change is to quit. It's an excuse to be lazy and not to help them. The changes I made in my life and see in the young people I coach and teach are profound.

Not everyone can be helped. And there are times when one cannot wait around for a change to present itself. Sometimes a kid must get cut, a friendship must end, an employee must be let go. But as a secondary level teacher and coach, I do not have the luxury of picking my students or players. If I want to win, I have to make the best of what I have to work with. If you can't hire an all-star team, then forge one out of the potential in the people you work with. Realize that a team of all-stars doesn't necessarily finish first. Why? Because they lack character and get beat by a bunch of overachievers; people with average talent who have made the best of it.

I have to help those I lead recognize that what I have to teach them in this regard will help them the rest of their lives. I have to do all I can to help them see how much they will benefit from growing their character and mental toughness. Sure, I teach them specifics related to the subjects and sports I am involved in. I also teach them general skills. More importantly, I teach them how to be winners. Once they learn how to win, they can win at just about anything. When a player or student realizes this, they are all in. I do little more than add some fuel to their tank and thus remind them and further inspire them. But they apply their own ever growing character and mental toughness and succeed at whatever they choose to do.

"Victorious warriors win first and then go to war,
while defeated warriors go to war first and then seek to win." –Sun Tzu

The quote above is often used to generate a concern for thorough strategic planning. One often ignored way to do this is to incubate and accelerate character and mental toughness development. Don't make your *modus operandi* the fixing of yourself and your people after a loss. Don't fail to be aware that today's victory was based on talent while tomorrow's challenge might require talent enhanced by strength in the traits. Don't be reactionary. Recognize the role the traits play in winning and then actively teach them to those around you long before the contest or due date.

You can't tell your daughter all she needs to know in the moment she departs for college. You would be much better off sending her away confident in the strength of character you consciously and actively instilled in her. So too is the preparation for the other big moments in our professional and personal lives. Long before we know the specific day our constituency will need a specific trait the most is precisely the time to foster character growth in your children, students, or employees.

When you lead by teaching people character and mental toughness as the basis of everything you and your organization do, then you can far better wager that the appropriate action will take place during that essential moment that determines success or moderate success, moderate success or failure. You need people who can make the play, or grind out the project in that moment that is going to make or break your organization. Make it a habit of teaching yourself and others the character and mental toughness needed to consistently win. Don't get upset because they didn't show "it" when things mattered most. Think about what you could have done better to help them see "it" long before. In constantly leading through the traits you will correct those costly flaws in character before it's too late.

"I saw the angel in the marble and carved until I set him free." – Michelangelo

There is much written about servant leadership. Well what better service could you provide as a leader than serving as a catalyst for the personal growth of those you serve; light their way. Have a discussion, share a link with them or give them a handout. Start small and then build from there. Put some fuel in their tank by putting some enlightened thoughts in their head. Watch as those who are stuck in doldrums begin rolling forward.

The Character Way holds up despite the diversity of our various struggles because of the commonality of human nature. No matter what you do, you have to deal with people, or at least yourself and you are a people too. One, a dozen, hundreds or more; we are people and we will ultimately succeed or fail largely based on our strength of character.

Martin Luther King Jr. so memorably discussed judging people on the content of their character. I am simply urging you to grow that very content in yourself and those you lead. Take something from this book or somewhere else. Share it with the people you lead. You will be doing them, and you, a service that could make a profound difference.

"The percentage of mistakes in quick decisions is no greater than in long-drawn-out vacillation, and the effect of decisiveness itself 'makes things go' and creates confidence"
- Anne McCormick

Gray or Grey? Even the spelling of the word is a gray/grey area. Apparently both are acceptable. You would think the etymology has to do with a shade of color between black and white, but I'm not so sure about this. I think the difference has more to do with indecisiveness and the inevitable lack of commitment; grey/gray.

I like dogs. For me that is enough to make my own personal decision and commitment on this issue. So I will choose grey as in greyhound. However, I do believe in tolerance, so please feel free to be as gray as you want and know that I will accept you for who you are.

Now that I have had my fun, let's get down to the purpose of this piece of the leadership puzzle. You can't lead from a grey area. You can effectively manage from a grey area, but you can't lead others or yourself. Grey means getting by, not getting better.

Leaders are black or white. They are decisive. They are committed. They follow through and make sure those they lead are accountable. Flexible black and white leaders will of course make adjustments along the way; but these adjustments are definitive as they directly relate to reaching the spoken goal.

Black and white leadership keeps the followers in mind. With a black and white leader you understand your goal and your role, and this makes it easier to commit to the vision. Because the vision is so clear, the leader so dependable, followers can make independent decisions. Followers trust that the leader will not change course with political expedience, so they commit and act with the goal in mind. Black and white leadership allows all parties to envision success and accountability. All parties will do whatever is necessary to achieve the goal. Efficiency, initiative and diligence are enhanced by black and white leadership.

Some in authority try to lead from a grey area. Grey leaders are indecisive. They do not follow through. They frequently change course when adversity or inconvenience are encountered. Followers have no firm idea where they stand or which direction they should go in. Grey leaders kill initiative because followers do not want to act if their actions will be irrelevant or unwise as the grey leader again changes direction. Grey leaders are not committed. They want things done, but they lack the resolve to follow through, to take a stand, to be held accountable. Grey leaders' sails are powered by the winds of political expedience as they navigate the path of least resistance; be it sometimes black, or sometimes white. Grey leaders stay afloat, but that's it. Grey leaders practice short term thinking that often is counter to accepted goals.

As in all things, there lies a good and a bad. The benefit of being a grey leader is that you seldom have anyone develop a negative view of you. The drawback of grey leadership, is that it seldom leads to notable achievement. It simply makes progress towards such notoriety unsustainable.

Choosing to be grey and preferring grey leadership are natural sorts of self preservation. People want to play it safe. They want to be secure. They want to avoid conflict. So they embrace and practice grey leadership. The only people who truly despise grey leadership are the people who aspire to progress and have the courage to endure the inevitable friction to achieve goals.

The black and white leader has the courage to risk and the mental toughness to endure. The black and white leader can fail, and fail miserably; but he can also attain greatness, which is something only fortune of circumstance can award a grey leader. The black and white leader can be despised; there are prices to pay for the mandatory decisiveness and accountability necessary to reach goals.

Now imagine if I had alternated between grey and gray throughout this piece. If that would have annoyed you, you are a black and white person. Now imagine if you had written this piece and had to submit it to two people who hold you accountable. The first you know prefers gray, so you changed every word to gray. The second prefers grey so you now change the word to grey. If this is your *modus operandi* you are a grey person. I will also add that if you are sometimes black and white and at other times grey, you are also a grey person.

With grey leadership, every experience is cloudy. This grey/gray is neither character nor mental toughness. It is evidence of the enemies of character, particularly justification and apathy. Grey leadership lacks commitment and heart.

If you truly want to accomplish notable personal or organizational goals, start thinking and acting in a black and white manner. Be decisive. Follow through. Commit the resources necessary to achieve the goal. Have the courage to accept the inevitable costs of progress.

When you lead The Character Way it becomes much easier to make decisions because so many of them can simply be viewed as The Character Way or The Easy Way. This has allowed me to practice black and white leadership. I set course to make this piece readable and memorable. I made a decision to go with grey. I showed a little courage as this may have been unpopular. I made the commitment and I followed through. Hopefully I achieved my goal and the picture is not fuzzy but clear. The Easy Way would have been to not share it all.

"The greater the obstacle, the more glory in overcoming it." –Moliere

One of the best statistics in sports is the plus/minus. Basically it determines how many goals or runs a team scores and gives up with a player in the game as opposed to how many are scored and given up with that player out of the game.

What about using plus/minus over a season? What difference does a player make to his team when he is there as opposed to when he is not? In a broader light, what difference does a person make when they are in someone's life as opposed to when they are not? I will leave that discussion for another day. The same principle can be employed when looking at any group of people who must work together.

Let's stick to the season perspective. Particularly, a couple of recent instances from the two sports I coach when a supremely talented player continuously displayed poor character and was ultimately removed from a team. Black and white leadership was demonstrated in each instance, because the coaches took The Character Way.

Going into the 2010 college football season Oregon quarterback Jeremiah Masoli was a leading Heisman Trophy candidate. Many spoke of how he was revolutionizing the quarterback position. On June 9, 2010, Oregon football coach Chip Kelly, one of my former coaches, dismissed Masoli from the team for his lack of character. On January 10,2011, Oregon played for the first time in the college football National Championship Game.

That Spring Virginia midfielder Shamel Bratton was a two-time All American and a leading candidate for the Tewaaraton Trophy, the highest award in collegiate lacrosse. Many spoke of how Bratton was revolutionizing the midfield position. On April 29 of 2011, Virginia lacrosse coach Dom Starsia dismissed Bratton from the Virginia lacrosse team for his lack of character. On May 30, 2011, Virginia played for the first time in five years in the college lacrosse National Championship Game.

There are some valuable lessons to be learned from these two recent situations. First, that you win leading The Character Way and not The Easy Way. Second, you win with winners.

Winners have the character and mental toughness to consistently do the work. They have character and mental toughness on and off the field, because that is who they are. Character and mental toughness are not something the winner turns off and on; it is something the winner becomes. No single star talent is better than the team. A person who refuses the opportunity to improve who they are is not worth our looking past The Character Way principles that are the foundation of winning teams. When the star talent gets in the way of the winning principles, it is the star talent that must go, not the winning principles.

Leaders make mistakes at this juncture all the time. Delayed gratification is more important than instant gratification. All of us, particularly leaders, must never lose sight of that. Simply put, don't think about what is going to be needed to win the game. Think about what is necessary to win the championship.

There will always be talented people who will never make the sacrifices needed to improve enough as people in order to win or even enough just to participate. This is a sad but true component of any endeavor.

"We are all in the same boat, in a stormy sea, and we owe each other a terrible loyalty."- G.K. Chesterton

The town I teach in is about 100 miles from Boston and 150 miles from New York City. I would say that 3/5ths of its citizens root for the Red Sox and 2/5ths root for the Yankees. However, in the other major sports the vast majority of residents root for the Patriots, Bruins, and Celtics rather than the teams based in New York City.

Why the difference in baseball? Well, I have found that you have to ask each person individually. When you do that, you get some interesting answers. You find out how they became loyal to their team. You also find that people seldom switch, become disloyal, and root for someone else.

What about their loyalty to other people? What about loyalty to the teams they play on? At what point do you become loyal to a person or a team or an organization? At what point do you become disloyal to a person or a team or an organization? In each situation, what is your loyalty point; the point where you become loyal or the point where you become disloyal?

Lately, we have encountered something I call "playing on the player's terms." This means that a player has little loyalty to the program or team they signed up for. The player feels he, or she, can come and go when it is convenient. A player can say "hey, I have a party to go to so I won't be practicing the next couple of days and I will miss a game." Or a player can say "I only want to play shortstop, so if you move me to the outfield I will quit." Or a player will blow off an entire winter and summer of weight training and still expect to start in the fall.

Some statements might help to clarify this "playing on the player's terms" mindset. I will sign up for football as long as I can play wide receiver or linebacker. I will show up for practice as long as I don't have something better to do. I will show up for practice as long as I don't have any sickness or pain. I will show up for practice as long as it's not too hot, or too cold. If our team starts losing, I will start bad mouthing them just like the people with no ties to the program. I will help out, or back the program if my son or daughter plays a lot. Are any of these loyal?

In many ways loyalty is the truest and most difficult test of character and mental toughness. This is because you have to be mentally tough not just for your own gain, but for the gain of another person or group.

So what causes a person to become loyal? I think it is the courage to love. At some point the loyal take the risk of falling in love. They fall in love with a sport, or a team, or a person. Their love allows them to be loyal.

What causes a person to become disloyal? I think it is love. At some point they fall out of love with a sport or a team or a person. For some people it takes a great deal for them to become disloyal, if they can be made to become disloyal at all. Others will become disloyal very easily.

What interests me is how much a person can take before they become disloyal. This is a measure of their character and mental toughness. For some it takes very little for them to become disloyal. For these people it is just a matter of simple convenience. For example one sport is just easy while another is difficult. You become loyal to the easy one. For others it is simply a matter of selfishness. For example one person you are newly friends with elevates your social status while a second person you have long been friends with does not. A disloyal person dumps the long time friend for the new one that elevates their status.

Why is loyalty important? Because it makes you dig deeper and sacrifice more than you could just for yourself. You become stronger and tougher, as you sacrifice for someone or something else, even when you don't want to. It eliminates the drama of outside distractions. When people speak poorly of your organization or team, your loyalty will prevent you from listening to them and thereby weakening your commitment and effort towards team goals.

If you want to become a great player you have to be loyal to your sport. That does not mean that you have to play only one sport. But it does mean hours of planning ahead and preparation and training to accommodate both. This means you will likely have to make some sacrifices. The more you are loyal to your sport, the more sacrifices you will make to prepare and train. The more loyal you are the more pain and discomfort and inconvenience you are willing to endure.

Loyalty is a two way street. Championship teamwork occurs as a result of loyalty. It occurs when each member of the team sacrifices for the others. It occurs when each member of the team gives the other members their best character. Championship teamwork occurs when we become tough enough to endure great inconvenience, pain, and discomfort because we are loyal to one another.

Loyalty is a risk. You may give your loyalty only to find out that your loyalty, or depth of loyalty is not returned. You may get burned as a result. But know full well that if you do not risk giving your loyalty, your deepest truest loyalty, then you will never get it back in return. All great teams have a few people with the courage to make this type of investment. Their example allows their teammates to begin to understand how such sacrifice leads to success. Loyalty inspires loyalty. Someone has to take the risk of being loyal first.

Loyalty defines your relationship. If you do not show your friends or your team how loyal you are, then don't be foolish enough to think they are going to be loyal to you! If your friends or team see that you are not willing to sacrifice for them, they will have very little interest in sacrificing for you. Yell and scream at them all you want, if you didn't lift and run and sweat with them, if you missed a week of practice, or avoided taking a hit, they could care less what you have to say.

We have discussed how to become loyal, but there are also times that you will need to become disloyal. Once you have given a person a few chances and found they do not take advantage of them, then maybe it's time to think about how loyal you should be. I think the best way to gauge this is by seeing if the other person or group helps you to become a better person. Not happy, or popular, or easy, but better.

On my bookshelves you will find more than a few works about coaches or public figures that remained loyal when they should not have. They stood by a player or valuable assistant when they clearly should not have. Misplaced loyalty can cost a leader his current position and even his legacy.

Loyalty is defined as being faithful to commitments or obligations, adherence to a designated structure, a sense of duty or attachment to someone or something. Loyalty is something you give, loyalty is something you get.

Nothing betrays your lack of loyalty as quickly as your negative comments (not to be confused with constructive criticism). Nothing demonstrates your loyalty as quickly as you helping someone get through a tough time. Being loyal means standing up for the person or group you are loyal to. Nothing tears your team or town apart more than a lack of loyalty. When the citizens or members spend more time ridiculing one another than sacrificing for one another, there will be little success. Your team or community will never have consistent success until they have consistent loyalty.

You want a truly great team, a truly great community; well here it is at its core! Let that first sacrifice be your mindset of initial support and let the second sacrifice be your simple gestures of selflessness. Let the third be your demonstration of mental toughness showing that you will not throw all the other life boat passengers overboard at the slightest wave, but rather will endure with them colossal towers of sea in the greatest of storms. Yes, you may get hurt, but you will never become the best until you have the courage to take that risk and sacrifice for others and the mental toughness to maintain that sacrifice and persevere when faced with adversity. Have the courage to raise your loyalty point with your fellow teammates and citizens and you just might find they raise their loyalty point with you.

Having high standards works if you stick with them, and people have the character and mental toughness to rise to meet them. Character amplifies talent. A lack of character diminishes talent. Character beats talent, when talent lacks character. If my team does not properly and frequently lift weights, they will remain weak. That takes character and I can't be the only one in my organization that knows that. I can't be the only one who expects that either. In instances where players or students forget about their character and mental toughness I will need other members of the team to remind them. I can't be everywhere or see everything our organization does. As such, peer on peer leadership is necessary.

I had a teacher pull me aside to tell me something. He told me he was walking down the stairwell one day while our players were training by running up the stairs. He said one of our younger players asked an older player if they were racing. The older player said "you are standing next to another man; what do you think?" I loved it! The older player brought his teammate up rather than having the younger one bring him down!

Another time that same week a player was squatting some pretty big weight. But their squats were not chair depth. One of his teammates spoke up and told the player he needed to squat to chair depth. An additional player then backed him up and said the same thing

Have you ever watched the TV show Super Nanny? It's funny because her teachings are effective and reinforce many of the things we incorporate with our team. She sets expectations and communicates those rules both verbally and in writing. She has a written schedule and she follows through with her expectations of people. You don't have to wear a tie or whistle to be a leader.

It's actually quite simple but hardly anybody does it right. Kids are smart. They know what they can get away with. Because kids are so used to people not following through with expectations, they sometimes take affront when they are actually confronted for not following through with things like being at practice on time or their failure to execute a technique in a game the way they were coached to do in practice.

In our program, if you are not where we ask you to be, doing what we ask you to do, you are very likely going to hear about it. Accountability is nothing more than leadership following through with the expectations of those they lead. Accountability is being held responsible for your actions on and off the field. You are coached to do something. You will be confronted if you do not do it.

For me the most important thing is not whether players will be held accountable for their decisions. No, the most important thing is who will hold the players accountable. When we are at our best as a team, a player or group of players hold themselves and the team accountable. Not the coaches.

I had a player we all called "Stick." When he had a season ending injury half way through our 2011 season, I had endless people comment to me that we would miss his play on the field. My response to virtually everyone was the same. "Sure he was a great player, but we have other good players. Our problem is that we will miss him in the huddle."

"Stick" took it upon himself to make sure our players were held accountable. When players were coached to do something to help the team be successful, then didn't do it, they were going to hear from Stick, before they even heard from a coach. And that wasn't always going to be pleasant. Especially if it was the same mistake being made over and over again or was caused by a lack of effort or focus. The tone on the team was set by Stick.

Players are given an assignment. They get it done to the best of their ability. If not, they are corrected. That is how you build winners and that's how a program consistently wins.

Stick would be as pleasant as he could be in trying to get his point across the first couple of times, but if you weren't paying attention he was not afraid of being unpleasant. That takes some awareness, initiative and courage.

When Stick went down, I talked to some other team leaders about taking on this role. They were very good leaders but maybe it just wasn't in their nature to hold others accountable as well as Stick did.

Then something changed, and to me it was the best moment of our season. We had a very difficult practice, and guys kept making mistakes. With every mistake the team was forced to do some bear crawls. Finally, after about a half an hour of this, the guys got their act together. They started to do well. Their confidence soared. However, later on near the end of practice, they once again started making mistakes over and over again.

Then one of the younger players spoke up, and let it be known that there would not be any further mistakes or players would have to answer to him. One of the seniors told him to calm down, and was shocked when the coaches supported the younger player instead of the older one. A couple of years later that younger player would subsequently lead us to a very successful and memorable season.

What the younger player had figured out was that if the team was to be successful the players needed to be accountable. Every single year we have been good, we have had a player who held the others accountable. These guys were willing to sacrifice being liked. Sometimes the guys on the team hated them. But I think every player on the team respected them. Every player on the team knew that these players were right. Every player on the team knew these players helped them to become better, and tougher. I call this role "The Answer Man" because this is the guy you have to answer to when you make mistakes that hurt the team.

This role takes a tremendous amount of character and mental toughness. The Answer Man must first demonstrate his own character. He has to be humble enough to show up and do the work alongside his teammates. This builds confidence in himself and in his teammates. He needs to show others that he knows he can get better too.

The Answer Man must also demonstrate toughness. This isn't a guy who misses. You need a couple tractors worth of horsepower to get him out of the lineup. He can dish it out, but more importantly he can take it. He can take a hit. He can take the pain. He can take whatever work gets thrown at him. He can take being corrected by the coaches.

The Answer Man needs to have an awareness of what needs to be done and recognize when it is not being done. The Answer man then has to have courage. The courage to speak up, even when he knows people won't like him; even when he knows that people will call him out when he makes a mistake. So he has to work twice as hard to make sure he doesn't give them an excuse to question his knowledge or desire or selflessness.

The Answer Man has to have initiative. Once he recognizes a problem he has got to try to solve it. He does so as nicely as possible. Teaching and explaining at first, but then getting stern if need be. Stern with a look or a word or a hit in a drill that makes his message clear.

The Answer Man must be consistent and willing to persevere. He can't quit being the Answer Man when he has a difficult day or his teammates won't listen. Once a team has an Answer Man, (or a couple of Answer Men) then ultimately it comes down to the team's willingness to listen.

Unfortunately, we have had a couple of years along the way where players refuse to follow the Answer Man. Maybe this is because they thought they were too good, or too special to do what is best for the team. Maybe they were too afraid to face their weaknesses. Maybe these players had never been called out before. Maybe these players were too busy feeling sorry for themselves to listen and grow. Those players never came close to reaching their potential and their teams were not nearly as successful as they might have been.

Every good team at any level or in any profession has an Answer Man, and people who will follow his lead. I will give you one more example. Patriots quarterback Tom Brady made his weekly appearance on the Dennis & Callahan show following a 34-27 victory over the Redskins. Brady got into a heated argument on the sideline with offensive coordinator Bill O'Brien after the QB threw a fourth-quarter interception. He chalked it up to the intensity of the situation. This is what Brady had to say, "We're both very emotional people, believe me. When things don't go so well, everyone gets frustrated. There's different ways that we express our frustration. When I make a play like that at the end of the game, it's not what any player/coach expects. That's just part of the game. He and I have a great relationship. Actually, I love that he feels that he can coach me. I think that's something as a veteran player you maybe don't get a lot from coaches. Because you're a veteran, you don't think, 'Aw man, I can't be yelled at.' But yeah, you can. And you should. We're all held accountable. Coach (Bill O'Brien) and I have a great relationship. I do that a lot, too. I get on guys all the time. It's a way to try to get guys to respond. Our team needs a lot of fire. We need a lot of emotion. That's the way you play the game."

People are only confronted if they are being bad; actually, really bad. I say this because on most occasions people will let bad just slip by so they can avoid a confrontation. They only assert themselves when they see truly obnoxious or abhorrent behavior. Confrontations require follow through. To confront without the willingness to follow through is a demonstration of weakness and only slightly better than lacking the character and mental toughness to confront at all. A leader must be willing to confront any negative behavior and have the strength of character to follow through until that behavior is changed. To avoid either is to lose the respect of those you lead as well as your peers and superiors.

People rarely slam their foot on the gas pedal to try to get someone to do better. To do so is considered poor form; as if it would be in violation of one's personal liberty to settle for mediocrity. But confronting a lack of effort is just as important as confronting detestable behavior. When my players lack enthusiasm and aggression I tell them that I would rather have to pull back their reigns than give them my spurs. But sometimes confrontation is needed to spur positive action and not just reign in negative behavior.

Many fail to recognize is that it is ok to confront someone to get better. As a result of this failing to confront each other about areas we can improve on, potential is wasted. We have to realize it is ok to confront one another, to push each other to do better, to call each other out when we are getting by instead of getting better. Such a push might not be appreciated in the moment, but it will be appreciated later as the person being confronted sees they could do more to fulfill their potential in helping themselves and others.

Properly executed confrontation isn't being mean. Being mean is standing idly by and watching someone do the wrong things; things that hurt themselves or their organization. Being mean is to watch people waste away their potential. If you do not have the courage to confront people, you are not doing them any favors. If you do not have the courage to accept confrontation, you are not doing yourself any favors.

So we really need to change two things. First, we cannot be afraid to confront someone to get them better. Second, when we get confronted, we have to be tough enough to handle it and see it as an opportunity to get better. Leaders set the example of proper confrontation and acceptance of confrontation.

In my early years of teaching, I had the great opportunity to be a teacher/counselor at a nationally recognized school for adjudicated boys outside of Philadelphia. There I was taught specific levels of confrontation, which I later adapted to my needs. The school had a prep school setting with no locks on the doors or bars on the windows, but it had some of the worst juvenile offenders in the country, including gang members from big cities who had committed the worst kinds of crimes.

But that school, and the unique program it utilized, took those kids and turned them from the worst to the best. These kids jumped years in grade levels on tests. They went on to college and got jobs in the trades. Not all of them of course, but the majority of them, which is amazing.

They changed because the people at the school understood what it took to be successful in life, understood that those kids had never been taught how to be successful, and refused to accept anything less than successful behavior.

The program was pretty simple. Students were told what they needed to do to be successful. If they were not doing the things they needed to be doing, they were confronted. Confronted by staff, and confronted by peers. Confronted one on one and confronted by the group. It was a way of life, and the results were dramatic. Not only were the students held accountable in such a manner, so were the staff members.

Being nice is important. You should always start confrontations in the nicest way possible, but then you should follow through with increasing levels until the confrontation is effective and the behavior is changed. Of course, you never want to do anything that will harm someone, and you also must recognize the times when you simply have to let a person be because the moment is not right, or they simply will never get "it."

I teach our team leaders how to confront their teammates. I also teach the rest of the team how to support and accept a confrontation. A confrontation is simply an attempt to change a negative behavior into a positive one. Remember the goal is not to punish, but to change the behavior. We confront because we want someone to stop taking The Easy Way and start taking The Character Way.

The Levels of Confrontation

1. **Friendly non-verbal.** Simply make eye contact with the person. This lets them know you are paying attention to them, which can be effective.
2. **Non-friendly non-verbal.** Give the person a look that lets them know you mean business. I'm sure my players and students know mine.
3. **Friendly verbal.** In the most pleasant way possible, let the person know their behavior needs to change. Talk to them. Explain the issues and behaviors that need changed, help them find a way to change it. Explain the positive and negative consequences of their behavior.
4. **Non-friendly verbal-** In a stern tone that lets someone know you mean business let the person know what needs change. Sometimes you need to get a little loud and serious in your tone.
5. **Touch for attention.** In a nice way, put your hand on someone's shoulder or tap their shoulder. If we have shoulder pads on you can give them a firm pat on the shoulder. If they resist this, take your hand back immediately. Some people are very sensitive to any type of contact.
6. **Active Reminders-** A reasonable amount of up-downs, sprints, rolls,

chutes, or bear crawls may be assigned to a player with the consent of the seniors. Seniors should first consult with a coach to make sure the amount and timing are appropriate. Players may also be assigned duties (shed, med kit etc.). If anyone is uncomfortable with an active reminder that has been assigned to them, then they don't do it and immediately speak with a coach and explain why they feel it would be inappropriate.

Support for Confrontation

It is very important that all of us be ready to support a confrontation. What do I mean by this? Let me give you an example. When a player is not hustling, and he gets confronted or "called out" by a teammate, the player not hustling may not listen and may become defiant. This is where the rest of the team comes in and supports the confrontation. All members of the team have to have the courage to stand up for what is important to our team and back someone doing a confrontation. Ever hear of "having someone's back?" This is a good example.

If someone needs support for a confrontation they simply turn to their teammates and ask for support by saying "Can I have support?" Their team is then obligated to either support the confrontation by saying "support" or not support it by saying nothing. It is important to mention that unsupported confrontations will result in the failure of the team. People will not confront other people if they know nobody has their back. We all have to have the courage to support appropriate confrontations.

Remember, the goal is to make ourselves and our team better. Confront if you see something needs to be changed. Follow the levels. Accept confrontation if you are confronted. Feel free to tell people "I accept your confrontation."

Support appropriate confrontation if you are asked to. Say "support" or repeat what was said. Not only do we need people to step up and be the "Answer Man," we also need the rest of us to understand that if we mess up over and over, we might need someone to call us out on it and we might need to pay a price to make sure we don't mess up again. Likewise, if we could be doing better for ourselves or our team, expect to hear about that too! Be humble and listen!

Final Thoughts on Confrontation

You may think that guys confronting each other all the time would lead to ill will or bad blood between them. But if everyone understands why confrontations take place, then something quite different happens. Teammates grow closer. Bonds become stronger. Brotherhood runs deeper. The reason for this is because confrontation forces interaction and reinforces focus on the means to our team goals. It lets us know we care about one another and we care about what we are trying to get done. It lets us know that both the people and the mission are truly important.

"If you could kick the person in the pants responsible for most of your trouble, you wouldn't sit for a month."- Teddy Roosevelt

I was discussing sarcasm the other day. I grew up in New Jersey. I went to college near Boston. It's ingrained in me. But I live in an area a little more removed; a place where sarcasm, symbolism, and satire are not well appreciated. I interact with a lot of literal people, so I am always guarded in my conversations as I don't want to hurt anyone's feelings. People who don't readily understand the three S's do understand tone, so I've learned to tamp down on my phrase play. It's not fun for anyone if nobody else gets the joke.

That discussion about sarcasm led to a point made by one of my former players from my early years of coaching. He said my players might not always understand me, but instead they did what I asked of them because they were afraid of me. I pondered that statement for a long time. I never set out to make anyone afraid of me. What I hoped he meant was that they feared I would hold them accountable.

Football isn't like all of the other sports. It requires relentless orchestrated physical contact. Players must be smart, strong, fast, quick, relentless, powerful, quick thinking, cooperative, responsible, disciplined, tough, etc. Those traits have to be developed and developed to a very high level in order to succeed. In football there are endless things to be held accountable for, but there are also endless things to take pride in. Football is accountability dependent and pride producing.

One must also understand that, unlike most of the other sports, in football you need a whole bunch of players who are willing to be held accountable and take pride in their efforts and performance. When things are not being done as instructed, then changes need to be made. When those changes are not executed, confrontation must occur. Otherwise, the unsuccessful behavior will continue and the individual and team will suffer.

A modern teacher or coach is accountable for the performance of their students or players. Statistics are kept on wins and losses, standardized tests passed and failed. However, when the teacher or coach now confronts the student when their behavior is not in keeping with the goals of instruction, the student, player, parent or supervisors no longer accept confrontation, or at least confrontation beyond the friendly verbal level. When my former player said he and his teammates did as told because they were afraid, something popped into my head. No Fear of Accountability = No Accountability = Failure to reach potential = Losing.

I can no longer hold students and players accountable if I don't have the ability to make them afraid of being accountable. I can't make them afraid if their parents fail to see any value in accountability. I can't make them afraid of accountability if the parent calls the supervisor and the supervisor does not support the method. There is no fear in the player or student under-performing if their parents or the supervisors don't have the ability to recognize the fruits of such confrontation.

Accountability creates a fear of failure and therefore avoidance of failure by increasing performance. This is what I was raised to believe and witnessed as being very effective in my early years of teaching and coaching. Whereas fear of being held accountable for poor performance used to motivate performance, now fear of being held accountable for negative performance leads people to fear participating at all. The player quits or won't challenge themselves and the parent, or supervisor supports the player's decision to take the easy way out.

If someone doesn't define failure and hold one accountable, then that individual will never develop the safety net of intrinsic pride which establishes a minimal acceptable level for achievement. In short, that someone never learns to do better and not accept failure.

As a teacher and coach, accountability, and the pride it leads to, requires courage; the courage of parents, teammates, coaches, and administrators. However, if one or more of those pillars lack the courage, the will, or the intellect to understand accountability, then there can't be accountability. This is because it won't be allowed. The result is any hope for a high level of performance is crushed.

The norm in some organizations or communities is that its members will hold each other accountable. This leads to consistent success. The norm in other organizations or communities is that its members will not be held accountable. This leads to consistent failure. There is of course a third norm where the level of permissible accountability fluctuates year to year, instance to instance. This leads to inconsistent achievement.

What does all of this mean? Well at some point, someone is going to ask me how we (our football team) are going to be next year. A great many factors go into whether we have a winning or losing season. Talent is a factor of course, but our talent is always pretty much the same. Administrative support is important, but that has been consistent.

See it doesn't really come down to me, or the talent level, or the administration. I've coached the program to some of the best seasons in school history, none of the worst, and plenty of the mediocre. I may not yell as much, or run them as much or make practices quite as grueling. I've changed a little bit because I've come to realize it's dependent on the character of the players and parents.

We will win if the players have some fear. We'll win if they have some pride and realize losing is unacceptable. We'll win if the players call each other out and listen when called out. We'll win if enough of their parents allow them to be held accountable so they can get the work done and develop some pride.

We'll lose if I solely have to hold our players accountable for doing every little thing (showing up to lifting, getting all their sets in, squatting to the appropriate depth, stretching with effort, handing in their paperwork, bringing out the water, finding a ride to camp, etc, etc.). We'll lose if more than the inevitable couple of parents start making phone calls and reach someone who holds no value of accountability and pride.

You see a high school football team never really resembles its coach, because the coach can't recruit or draft from anywhere he chooses. He only gets to coach the kids in that community. Instead a football team represents the parents, the players, the administrators, and ultimately the community that it evolves from and represents.

Those communities vary in their approach to accountability, and therefore vary in their level of pride and success. Some win all the time, some never win, and others win some and lose some. This is one very important reason why different communities or organizations with similar levels of talent consistently win, while others consistently lose, and still others are forever vacillating between the two.

Each year I need to help the football players who will be seniors learn the basics of leadership. In doing so I developed an acronym that provides six keys to leadership. I like the word direct. I like how it is an active word that means to conduct or tie together. I like how it implies the shortest most efficient route through timeliness, hustle, and relentlessness. I also like that it is black and white and not grey.

The Six Keys of Direct Leadership

1. <u>Destination</u>. You have to figure out which port your group is trying to reach. Leaders set the goals. You must examine the resources at hand and determine the means of achieving the goal. Work backwards from the goal and put together a map of the steps that are needed to take place in order to reach it. Share the relevant information about the goal and your vision for achieving it. The destination drives the destiny. The destination determines the day.

2. <u>Initiative.</u> You must adopt a mindset that nothing will get done without your active effort. Foster in others both awareness and self motivation. You have to encourage the group to see what needs to be done in order to achieve the goal. You must encourage them to take action on their own and do what needs to be done without being told. You must look for and recognize this self-starting and self-motivating ideal. You must accept that it will not always be perfect. Sometimes rewarding a display of initiative is far more important than deciphering the appropriateness of the action that

was taken. Initiative is a high level asset that requires awareness, courage, and commitment.

3. Redirect. You must keep the group on task. The minute the leader lets up, so will everyone else. The leader must be the most focused and driven member of the team. The leader must provide the discipline for others and prove his or her own self-discipline. While the leader may need to adapt along the way, and adopt methods conducive to getting the most out of the group, the leader must always have the destination first and foremost in his or her mind. The course may change, the destination should not.

4. Evaluate. A group member may vary in their level of character and mental toughness from day to day. Group members will vary in their level of commitment. Evaluate the group. Evaluate the progress toward the goal. Evaluation leads to proper preparation as it reveals pace and positioning as related to the goal.

5. Communicate. Listen. Broaden the means of communication so that each member has an opportunity to both speak and listen in a format that they are most comfortable. Listen and observe at least twice as much as you speak. The group members will be more sensitive to the tone of your communication then they will be to the actual words you use.

6. Teach. Remember the teachers you learned best from; the ones in and out of school. Not your favorites per say, but the ones you learned the most from. Adopt their techniques. Leave people better for having worked with you.

In order to consistently lead people to success one must demonstrate humility in showing others that they recognize room for their own improvement. A leader must show he cares about reaching unit goals and the people helping him in that journey. He should make obvious his diligence and ability to work with others. He should show his mental toughness by making character driven choices under pressure. He teaches those traits to his subordinates so that the quality, intensity, and duration of their work reach potential. In doing so he also imparts important lessons into the pursuit of everyday tasks making the work more profound and meaningful for all involved.

Leading through character and mental toughness provides a basis for clear, consistent, and timely decision making. This increases efficiency and initiative while building faith in the current mission and the direction of the organization. The character example and mental toughness of action allows the leader to hold those he leads accountable while allowing them to accept accountability as an instrument for improved production. Leading The Character Way prevents many problems that emerge when organizational members take The Easy Way and helps to extinguish those problems when they do surface. The Character Way leader has the awareness to know when to lead, follow or get out of the way.

15
AWARENESS

"Not here and there, but everywhere,
Be wise and ware:
No sharper steel can warrior bear."- Cicero

Everything you do or don't do is a test of your character and mental toughness; everything. Those who don't know become apparent to those who do. Stump the clinician is a game played by the oblivious at clinics or seminars where someone who is unaware tries to let everyone know how aware they are. It's an ironic game. Awareness means knowing what is going on around you. It involves all kinds of things, like the weather, the time left on the clock, the feelings and thoughts of others, and what's at stake if you lose. These are some of the endless variables which contribute to success and failure. To be aware is to recognize a great many of them and then act accordingly. Having awareness allows one to make decisions quickly while thinking long term. Awareness combines all of the other character traits. Because of this, awareness is the highest level of character.

I have some talents. One of which is my ability to argue. I have seldom lost a war of words. I used to mock my mother telling me "just because you're right doesn't mean you're right." When it came to our differences I didn't lose many bouts. Later on in life I found myself doing the same with my wife. I would win the argument, but that didn't make our marriage any better. It was only then that I came to realize that the abilities to make a point, to justify, to defend, and to manipulate do not necessarily make a situation better. In short, I became aware.

Awareness can be viewed in a couple of ways. One way to look at it is to look at people who are aware. When I think of awareness I think of a few people. One fictional, the others very much flesh and blood.

The first is the character Neo in the Matrix movies. Throughout the first installment, Neo has his doubts about his place and identity. Gradually he gains knowledge, skills, and confidence. He grows increasingly aware.

In the final battle of the first movie in the trilogy, Neo conquers the unbeatable foe, Mr. Smith. Neo does this when he sees things as they are. This is far different than his very limited initial perceptions. Neo has summoned all of his new found knowledge and skills. His OODA Loop, the ability to digest information and make appropriate decisions expediently, is so well developed and his perceptions are so clear, that he sees the 1's and 0's of The Matrix.

When I see consistently successful people, both near and far, what I see are those that have grown their character and mental toughness to the point where they can see the 1's and 0's of life. Every situation, every issue, every problem or circumstance boils down to these 1's and 0's. The aware person can identify them and take the appropriate action, while those around him seem rather mystified.

I see this ability develop in my best players and students. Not the ones with the most talent, but the ones who are the best people. They seem to not only have the answer; they also know why others don't. The same holds true of the great leaders of history. This is because they have developed their character and mental toughness to the level of awareness.

Until a person develops those qualities, and lives their life in accordance with them, they will remain unaware of their potential, their influence, the needs of others and the connections between past, present, and future. They will be unaware of near and far, the minutiae and the big picture. They will stay unaware of how lessons and concepts can be applied across fields. They will continue to be oblivious of the reasons for success and failure across the broad array of human experience.

The unaware will make bad decisions and mistakes which will cost themselves and others; often in ways they will never understand. To be aware is to see the 1's and 0's everywhere and in everything. The great ones have this ability. Part of their ability allows them to see The Character Way or The Easy Way.

The second person I will use as an example was an idol of my youth. He succeeded in his professional and personal life. He had his flaws and made mistakes, some have been recently documented. But he was human, not a work of fiction.

He was nicknamed "Sweetness" for his kind and generous demeanor outside of competition. But he was also known for his relentless and fearless physicality as a player. Chicago Bears Hall of Fame running back Walter Payton is remembered as an explosive competitor and gentleman. He learned to compete at an early age growing up playing sports against his older brother, who also later played in the NFL.

Some of his runs in the NFL are among the best of anyone who ever played. For most of his career he played on poor teams and only made one Super Bowl. He retired with almost every rushing record in the NFL including most yards in a career and game. Although he gained all those yards, he was better known for never giving an inch.

He died at an early age (45) of cancer. But in my opinion he was the greatest football player who ever lived. He may not have been the greatest running back, but he was the greatest football player. He may have also been the greatest person to play football who ever lived. Not due to his talent, but due to his awareness. He saw more of what was going on around him than normal people do. Not just on the field but off it. The NFL has an annual Walter Payton Award honoring one player as Man of the Year for his volunteer and charity work.

Payton was mentally tough. He only missed one game in his 13 year career. He never missed a practice. He was caring. He not only gave his money, but his time to many charities in Chicago. Payton was always nice to the people around him, including his opponents after a play was done. He made a point to befriend the younger players even though he knew some of them wouldn't last. He knew the names of the custodians and secretaries and made sure to ask them about their lives so they would know he appreciated their efforts too.

He was humble. Although he took pride in his performance, he always gave credit to his teammates and family. He learned the systems of new coaches that came in and mastered new techniques. He flipped the ball to the ref when he scored rather than draw attention to himself. He sacrificed his body blocking to the extent that he helped a teammate rush for 1,000 yards in the same season that he did; a rare feat in football.

He was responsible. He knew his plays. He took care of his family. He knew people looked up to him and he avoided situations that led to problems with substances or the law.

He was loyal and optimistic. He always gave the Bears and his teammates his best. It took ten years for his team to reach the Super Bowl, but he never complained, or demanded a trade. Instead he gave a great effort every Sunday and worked hard in practices and games.

He was committed and had initiative. He came to the professional level from a very small college and had to prove he belonged in the NFL to achieve his dream. Long before players worked out in the off-season, Payton was known to run a dirt path that was almost a mile long and very steep over and over. This was Mississippi in the summer time. He was disciplined.

He had courage. Payton was a fierce competitor and would often run over defenders trying to tackle him. He did this even though he was small by NFL standards. He rarely ran out of bounds at the end of the run, choosing instead to dish out a hit rather than avoid one.

Payton was the most complete running back to ever play football. He was an excellent blocker, receiver, and even threw for touchdowns a couple times a year. When his quarterback would throw an interception it was often Payton who made the tackle. Walter Payton was aware that he had to make sacrifices in order for his team to be successful. He knew teamwork was important.

In 1985, at the end of his career, Payton's Bears made the Super Bowl and whipped the Patriots 46-10. Even though his team had the ball on the one- yard line towards the end of the game, his coach decided someone else should score the touchdown. His teammates told Walter not to worry about it, that he would score when the Bears got to the Super Bowl the next year. Walter made them aware that they may never get back to the Super Bowl; that every day counted and should be used to its fullest.

The Bears did not make the Super Bowl again for another 20 years; long after Payton had retired and passed away. But Payton was aware of those around him, he was aware that his playing career and even his life would not last forever. As a result, he made sure to maintain great character every day and became the greatest and most respected player to ever play the game.

When it came time for Payton to be inducted into the NFL Hall of Fame, it was his son Jarrod who joined his father in giving memorable speeches during the induction ceremony. Payton's legacy exceeded his football exploits. A fine family, every bit the representation of his life as the bronze bust placed in the hall.

Another example is Martin Luther King Jr. The final night of his life was an amazing example of awareness. He was aware of his past the day before he had seemingly bailed on a civil rights march in support of striking garbage workers in Memphis. He was aware that some people thought him a charlatan and coward for not standing defiant in the face of violence that erupted during the march. He was aware of the moment. Just as he had done in Washington less than five years earlier in delivering his "I Have a Dream" speech, he went off script and spoke from the heart to address the needs of the people before him. His "Mountain Top" speech was equally memorable and poignant in addressing perceptions from the previous day and the needs of the moment. He saw the big picture, and the detail. He tied the past and present. He was aware of the thoughts and needs of others. He was aware of the future, as evident in the certainty of his predictions of success for the civil rights movement, and his inexplicable premonition of his own impending death only a few hours later.

The final example is one of my former players. It is rare to witness the manifestations of a young man's will over an extended period. That translation of thought sparked by a directed desire and then maintained by a vigilant and disciplined work ethic. While many young men are capable of flashes of brilliance, few can sustain this affect. In 2006, on a Friday night, I ran from the sidelines to the forty-yard line where Ryan was lying on the field. His eyes watered but his jaw was clinched in refusal, as to not let anyone know the pain he was truly in. I saw what had happened to his leg. It was grotesque. I thought he would never play another sport again.

He was out of school for a couple weeks. He was wheel chair bound for a few more. But by the middle of basketball season he was trying to run through basketball drills and eventually would start a few varsity games. By baseball season he had regained some speed. In the summer he ran hills and lifted weights on his own. He made it through a football camp or two.

In August he set the record for the forty-yard dash. In November he ran for 300 yards and five touchdowns against the opponent that had broken his leg a year earlier, even though he now had two broken hands. Ryan also earned the highest grade point average on the team as he led them to post-season play for the first time in twenty years.

The epitome of leadership is to get people from point "A" to point "B" in an efficient manner despite the group's potential and regardless of whatever adversity is encountered. Ryan did that in leading his team to the playoffs for the first time in twenty years. He had all the character traits of a great leader. His courage, discipline, responsibility and initiative were clearly evident. His integrity was unique for someone his age. He was loyal to his peers and coaches, yet was not afraid to voice his own opinion. But he also had the trait that is rare even among leaders. He had amazing awareness. He had an innate ability to grasp all of the variables in a given situation. That ability allowed him to make timely and effective decisions to put himself and his constituents in the best position to succeed. He had tremendous focus but he combined it with broad perspective.

Ryan clearly demonstrated intrinsic motivation for personal success. But what I found most amazing about Ryan was that his own success was subservient to any shared success he had with his team. It's almost as if Ryan knew he was capable of achieving any goal he put his mind to; and as such enjoyed an even higher satisfaction that comes only from helping others; albeit his team, individual teammates, his school, or community to achieve their goals. He was selfless. He would readily make any personal sacrifice for the greater good.

Ryan graduated from one of the finest colleges in New England. He was a three year all-league player. He would come back during our last practice before our big Thanksgiving game to say hello to the coaches and share a brief word with the team. On Youtube there is a video of him adeptly playing southern rock guitar, gladly accompanying his little sister, an aspiring singer. He "gets it." He is simply the best kind of man;

the kind with character and the mental toughness to be counted on in any situation.

16
AWAKENED

"No society can prosper if it aims at making things easier, instead it should aim at making people stronger!!" — Ashoka

When you see each decision as simply taking The Easy Way or The Character Way, life makes much more sense and people more efficiently read. The Easy Way is the path of least resistance; the path water takes when you spill it on a table. The Easy Way requires little or no effort. It is difficult to convince people of the merits of The Character Way. Unfortunately, we are decidedly inclined to believe one group of people more than any other; .the group that offers us the easiest path. Most people try to take The Easy Way, until they discover it does not work. Then, if they are competitive enough, they will travel The Character Way which will lead them to success. The quicker they give up The Easy Way and take The Character Way, the quicker they will be successful.

We make hundreds of decisions a day; if you really want to get better each choice comes down to one is easy, and one is difficult but gets you better.

Everyone affiliated with our football program has the same goal. Parents, students, teachers, administrators, alumni, and the community at large all want the same thing from our program. They want to see us win games and produce fine young men. So if everyone wants the same thing, why are there conflicts within the program? Why do we have frustrations between parents and their sons, coaches and players, players and players, coaches and parents, parents and parents?

I believe there are two sources of frustration. The first source of conflict is related to communication. That issue has been addressed elsewhere. The second source of conflict is the approach we take towards achieving our common goal. We all want to get to the same place but we differ on how to get there. The proposed routes to our common goal can roughly be boiled down to this: The Character Way or the Easy Way.

Most people choose The Easy Way, at least on occasion. Usually it is their first course of action. They do this for one of three reasons. They do not know any better, they do not give any forethought to their decision, or they care solely for themselves. The Easy Way is the simple obvious path that takes little or no effort and gives the person taking it little or no pain.

Those without courage take the simplest Easy Way which is to quit by never trying or to try some and then quit once things become uncomfortable. For example, these people rarely play high school football or stop playing after freshmen year. Instead, they often join activities that require less character and mental toughness. Some may excel and ultimately fulfill their potential but it will never come until they truly challenge themselves. Many will never venture outside of their comfort zone.

Those who are immature believe that The Easy Way will lead them to comfort, and prosperity. They believe someone will take care of them and that they will never have to take care of themselves. They feel like things will always be given and never have to be earned. Most people eventually grow beyond this, but not until they are forced to earn their accolades and take care of themselves.

All the same, some who have courage and are mature still take The Easy Way. Their Easy Way theoretically leads to their child, department, company etc, receiving comfort, attention, accolades, wealth, or popularity. Oxymoron or not, this is vicarious selfishness. People who take this path, and the people who encourage them, have great difficulty seeing anything wrong with taking this route. After all, their character seems altruistic as it is directed at someone or something else. Most others instinctively realize there is something wrong with this, but as instincts are things we know but cannot as of yet articulate, they have trouble identifying that this is just selfishness by proxy. It layers glory on that one person or organization they care about. Like Khufu's driving thousands to their deaths to build the Great Pyramid, their Easy Way still requires that everyone else sacrifice but not for the common good.

Seldom does The Easy Way work out. Usually it ends in failure and regret. The person who takes The Easy Way fails. Their failure is that they do not reach their full human potential. The Easy Way may win in one instance but it does not teach the person the keys to true success. True success can be repeated. The means to true success can be applied to all types of situations, not just the one situation where the person may have rare natural talent or total guidance and support.

If you take The Easy Way you also fail others. It robs others of the opportunity to interact with your best self, your positive example, your caring and kindness and selfless generosity. It robs them of feeling like they should become a person of character like you. It robs them of feeling like they should help you become better as well.

Sometimes your taking The Easy Way unfortunately encourages others to look out for number one and take The Easy Way too. It deprives everyone of the opportunity to share in true success as a team or community. People end up surviving alone or in their small group, rather than thriving together as a team.

Sometimes The Easy Way actually works out; the person achieves the goal and gets the glory. However, when The Easy Way works out, it is usually because someone has rare talent (athletic, intellectual, social) or has manipulated the contest in their favor (cheated, fooled, coerced), or has been incredibly fortunate.

The person who succeeds taking The Easy Way eventually gets revealed. The opponent's maturity or their hard work allows them to match the person or team that took The Easy Way and temporarily succeeded. The person or team that succeeded taking The Easy Way tops out with their natural ability or has their deceptive methods discovered.

The person who takes The Easy Way cannot repeat success in other areas of their life. The person who takes the Easy Way later regrets they did not grow when they had the chance. They never learned to become all they can be. They never became a person who can be counted on in any situation. They never came close to reaching their potential.

Examples of The Easy Way are all around us, because many people take The Easy Way and therefore confuse it with true success. There are endless subtle examples but here are some obvious ones.

Think of the individual who reaches the heights of political power, only to have it revealed he cheated on their taxes, or their bar exams, their resume or their family.

Think of the basketball, lacrosse, or hockey player who beams with pride after a game because he has scored a bunch of times, but fails to recognize that his team lost because this great scorer didn't play any defense or didn't get his teammates involved in the offense.

Think of the coach who fails to take out the star player for doing something unsportsmanlike because he is afraid of losing the game, yet the player does the same thing later on in an important moment of the championship game and the team loses.

Think of the student who asks her peer, who has the same math class a previous period, about the questions on that day's math test. The student gets an "A"" on that particular test, but hasn't learned anything that will help her later on her SAT's, the state tests or in her job interviews.

Think of the professional athlete who is a genius on the field or court or ice, but can't stay out of trouble in the real world and has little of value to show for their career once they stop playing.

"The bitterest tears shed over graves are for words left unsaid and deeds left undone. "
-Harriet Beecher Stowe

Instinctively The Easy Way leads to a sense of anxiety and even impending doom. It makes the person who takes it nervous because they instinctively know that they will ultimately have regret for not following The Character Way. The Easy Way offers immediate gratification but no prolonged solace. The person who takes it, even if they reach their goal, feels no lasting sense of satisfaction.

In contrast, the person who takes The Character Way has a profound sense of peace. They feel fulfilled that they have been their best self. They know that they can count on themselves to make the best of any situation. They know other people can count on them. They feel connected by the fact that they have made others better and allowed others to make them better. They feel like the traveler after a long and challenging trip. They may not have reached their destination, but they have learned so much along the way that their journey has surely been worthwhile. They have the confidence one only gets from having the courage to be out of their element, in order to discover and overcome their character weaknesses. They tend to sleep well at night unless of course they are too energized by the thought of the challenges of a new day.

The enemies of character are ignorance, apathy and justification. Avoid them at all costs. All will slow a person or group's character development, or erode the character they have worked so hard to earn. Never underestimate the capacity of people to choose The Easy Way and justify their choice.

This is why character is so rare. It is much easier for people to not care, not summon their enthusiasm, and make or take excuses. All three enemies will try to drag a person or group back to being average or stop them from ever attempting to reach their potential in the first place. One must be ever vigilant against the appearance of these enemies in our words, in our actions, and in our minds.

"The best portion of a good man's life is his little, nameless, unremembered acts of kindness and of love" —William Wordsworth

The Character Way or The Easy Way

The Easy Way is to look at something from the near side.
The Character Way is to examine all sides.

The Easy Way is to be indifferent.
The Character Way is to make a difference.

The Easy Way is to make fun of others.
The Character Way is to include others in the fun.

The Easy Way is to pay attention when being entertained.
The Character Way is to pay attention when being educated.

The Easy Way is to be the hero in the video game.
The Character Way is to just be in the real game.

The Easy Way is to mope over disappointment.
The Character Way is to accept, hope for better, and move on.

The Easy Way is to be the toughest in the softest crowd.
The Character Way is to hold your own amongst the toughest crowd.

The Easy Way is to ask a favor.
The Character Way is to recognize when someone is doing you a favor.

The Easy Way is to build self esteem by praising the average.
The Character Way is building pride by conquering the arduous.

The Easy Way is to talk.
The Character Way is to listen.

The Easy Way is looking for outs.
The Character Way is looking for opportunities.

The Easy Way is to make mistakes.
The Character Way is to make amends.

The Easy Way is to sip, stuff, dip, or puff.
The Character Way is saying enough's enough.

The Easy Way is to cheat and get an "A"
The Character Way is to do the work and earn a "B"

The Easy Way is to forget the needs of others.
The Character Way is to treat all like brothers.

The Easy Way is to stay put.
The Character Way is to be still.

The Easy Way is last one in, first one out.
The Character Way is first one in, last one out.

The Easy Way is to react with emotion.
The Character Way is to act with composure.

The Easy Way is to say the rules.
The Character Way is to set the example.

The Easy Way is to stand in the spotlight.
The Character Way is to shine your light on others.

The Easy Way is to sleep and dream at night.
The Character Way is a dream that makes you fight your fight.

The Easy Way is to get there first.
The Character Way is to make sure others get there too.

The Easy Way is stealing.
The Character Way is steeling.

The Easy Way is the talent you were born with.
The Character Way is the ability you earned.

The Easy Way is to be late for class.
The Character Way is the class to be on time.

The Easy Way is to avoid the pain of current self-discipline.
The Character Way is to foresee the pain of future self regret.

The Easy Way is to celebrate when you win.
The Character Way is to learn from those who beat you.

The Easy Way is to do what comes naturally.
The Character Way is to do what makes you better.

The Easy Way is "I will tomorrow."
The Character Way is finding the will today.

The Easy Way is to understand you need to work hard.
The Character Way is to work hard.

The Easy Way is to check your phone.
The Character Way is to check your phone at the door.

The Easy Way is the initial path that leads you downhill.
The Character Way are the first steps that lead you to great heights.

The Easy Way is to complain.
The Character Way is to comprehend and offer a solution.

The Easy Way is to rest like all the rest.
The Character Way is to do the work unique to the best.

The Easy Way is to enjoy life every day.
The Character Way is enjoying our daily strife.

The Easy Way is to hit the chips and couch.
The Character Way is to hit the treadmill and weights.

The Easy Way is to make promises.
The Character Way is to make progress.

The Easy Way it is to claim you couldn't get a ride.
The Character Way it is to walk however far it takes.

The Easy Way is to look for a job.
The Character Way is to realize you already have one.

The Easy Way is to say we care.
The Character Way is to know to show it every day.

The Easy Way is to say it's not your turn.
The Character Way is realizing the extra turn will do you some good.

The Easy Way is to sit in the stands and be a genius.
The Character Way is to step foot on the field and be genuine.

The Easy Way is to learn from your mistakes.
The Character Way is to learn from the mistakes of others.

The Easy Way is the best in your town.
The Character Way is the best in all around.

The Easy Way is to do whatever you want relying on others to control you.
The Character Way is being able to discipline and control yourself.

The Easy Way is to think about improving.
The Character Way is improving.

The Easy Way is to think of ways to benefit from others.
The Character Way is to think of ways to benefit others.

The Easy Way is to drop something on the floor and pretend it's not yours.
The Character Way is to pick something up knowing it's not yours.

The Easy Way is to love the lovely.
The Character Way is to see the beauty in all.

The Easy Way it is to go home and turn on the tv.
The Character Way it is to go for it and turn on your metabolism.

The Easy Way is to make fun of something that challenges you.
The Character Way it is to accept the challenge.

The Easy Way is getting by in all you do.
The Character Way is getting better in all you do.

The Easy Way is trying things on until you find the perfect fit
The Character Way is rocking what you have on.

The Easy Way is to want everything.
The Character Way is to make the best of anything.

The Easy Way is to complain that someone is being too tough on you.
The Character Way is to get tough enough that others complain about you.

The Easy Way is easy now and difficult later.
The Character Way is difficult now and easy later.